My Horse Told Me:

Everyday communication with your horse

CADMOS

Contents

Contents

Dedicated to Mali, my Fjord mare – everything began with you. You made my life!
(Photo: Karen Diehn)

Foreword

In today's equestrian world there are countless books and papers about how to ride and the effect a rider can have on their horse. These debate at length how the aids should be given in order for the horse to react in the desired way. By comparison there is unfortunately very little written about the signals that the horse is giving out to the world around it, to its fellow horses and also to the people around it.

In this work Daniela Bolze and Christiane Slawik have gone a step further. They attempt to help the motivated horse owner and rider to recognise and correctly interpret the signals that his or her horse is sending out, not just when being handled from the ground but also when being ridden.

To a certain extent the first signs of many of the problems that might lie ahead can be picked up by carefully observing any horse. The tossing of the head, swishing of the tail and frantic chewing aren't always necessarily a sign of resistance or disobedience, but rather are often caused by a poorly fitting saddle, poorly maintained teeth or a rider's flapping legs or heavy hands.

In the circus world the careful observation of equine behaviour has special significance. As soon as a trainer selects a horse to perform liberty dressage they must be able to see immediately which animal will fit into which position in the routine and for which exercise a horse may have a special talent.

Daniela Bolze has been teaching on the subject of "equine language" for many years and she passes on her knowledge to interested riders and owners with sensitivity and understanding.

Having a perception and awareness of a horse's character and state of mind is of vital importance if you want to be successful in training. A horse will feel more "understood" and will thank its rider by being more cooperative and performing to its full potential.

We hope that this book reaches a wide readership that, after working through the book, will have learnt that many misunderstandings can be avoided by simply looking and listening. Only then can a horse owner become a horse expert – for the good of all horses.

Ina Krüger-Oesert and Gino Edwards

Ina Krüger-Oesert is a well-known performer and has been giving seminars on classical Baroque dressage, working in-hand and circus tricks for 20 years. In 2009 she won an award from the German Equestrian Federation for her highly trained Spanish horses in her riding school which strives towards a higher level of leisure riding.

Gino Edwards is descended from a long-established circus dynasty and is particularly well known for his liberty act using six Arab stallions. He was one of the directors of the legendary equestrian musical "The Magic Forest" (performed extensively throughout Continental Europe) and has made a name for himself as a capable and sensitive trainer in seminars and courses.

Many people wish their horses could have such a beautiful loose box in such a magnificent stable, but is it really what an animal that originates from the steppes of Asia needs or really wants?

Two worlds colliding

There have never been as many horse owners as there are today. And never before has a horse had so few points of contact with our day-to-day life as now. This is an unhappy combination out of which it is the horse that suffers most of all. The fact that we have no regular experience of, or contact with, horses as part of our daily life means most significantly of all that we don't, as a matter of course, "pick up" valuable information about horses' behaviour or character. This is quite different from earlier generations, where the horse still played a significant role in both agriculture and transport.

Personally, I was very lucky that in the yard where I learnt to ride from the age of ten "Grandpa" Lübbers looked after all the horses. Although a man of few words he was a likeable East Prussian of indeterminate years – to us children he seemed to be at least 100 years old – who had not only seen Trakehners when they were still in the State stud in the town of Trakehnen but who had also been a part of their flight to the West during the Second World War. He was often seen to raise his eyebrows when he saw how the slightly more eccentric owners handled their horses. In the care of his large quiet hands the most insecure of animals settled down and could be handled. It was Grandpa Lübbers' silent example that planted the first seeds that led me to realise that calmness, respect, knowledge and a great deal of commitment was a part of any relationship with horses – something that my riding instructor had not made clear to me. During riding instruction it was always a matter of applying the right aids, driving the horse forward, bending, flexing and riding the correct movements. It was Grandpa Lübbers who taught me real horse sense in terms of the day-to-day contact with our friend the horse.

We have written this book in an attempt to revive and restore some of this knowledge that has been largely lost to the past.

We would like to raise the readers' awareness of and encourage them to look more carefully at their horses and for each reader to develop a better feel for his or her own horse and for its own individual language and way of expressing itself. It would be wonderful if the result of this greater level of observation led to a better level of understanding between horse and owner – with fewer misunderstandings and more enjoyment, harmony and also successes. We would like to call upon everyone to go to their own yard not just to ride, but instead for a change simply to observe. Don't just experience your horse when it is in its stable, but take time to observe it with other horses out in the field.

In my riding school I have used Christiane's photos in many of my theory lessons when teaching the children about equine behaviour. They catch certain moods and patterns of behaviour that my own ponies tend not to show always – thank goodness, when I think about some of the aggressive behaviour that these photos illustrate. It is however very important to be able to identify some of this behaviour so as to be able to recognise when things may be getting potentially dangerous. On Christiane's website I was able to rummage through photos showing horses expressing themselves and showing a wide range of feelings and it was this that led to the idea of a jointly written book.

I hope from the bottom of my heart that the following pages open the way to you finding the path to your horse's real character. And even more, it proves the fact that you are interested in the subject – as otherwise you wouldn't be reading this at all...

Christiane Slawik
with a grateful
model.

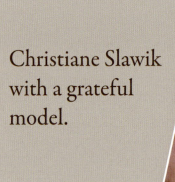

This is what I enjoy the
most: being free and at one
with my mare, Mali.

(Photo: Karen Diehn)

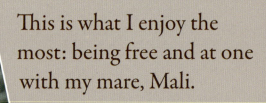

Why we have written this book

I have had the unbelievable luck of being able to live in close proximity to my horses and ponies for nearly 20 years. I not only look after my own horses, but also train them. Since 2004 I have run a successful riding school primarily for children and young people in which I don't just teach them the technical aspects of riding but also show them how to build a healthy and happy relationship with their horses. This includes how to read their horses' body language, how to lead, groom, recognise and treat certain illnesses as well as how to look after and feed them. I am assisted in all of this by my 18 four-legged teachers – wonderful ponies and horses with 18 different personalities ranging from Shetland foals to Koniks, Fjord ponies to Andalusians and warmblood crosses. In addition, thanks to having a range of client's horses as well as my own, I have a chance to interact with many other types and breeds that I don't happen to have in my home herd. I am therefore in the position of earning my daily bread by observing horses before, during and after lessons for many hours a day so that I can instruct my pupils appropriately. As I am together with animals from early until late on a daily basis I also get to witness all of the facets of a horse's daily life. I just can't get enough of simply watching them out in the field over the fence. New games and play groupings, the mood of the herd, expressions of joy and annoyance – I find all of this more gripping than reading a thriller. And I'm not alone in putting this book together. Alongside me is the well-known equine photographer Christiane Slawik. For decades she has travelled the world and photographed horses of every breed. Over the years she has learned to "listen" with her eyes and as a result catches the most magical of moments which is what make her pictures so unique. She can describe this much better herself:

"Much of what I have seen and photographed as a photo-journalist on so many continents and in so many diverse cultures puts our own very Western-oriented view of horses into perspective. We think that we do everything with horses perfectly. How presumptuous are we? Is a top, overfed competition horse that spends 23 hours in its box really any better off than the thin horses that service the tourists around the Pyramids of Giza but who are at least in the company of their owners all day? Although fed and well cared for, the former is sentenced to lifelong imprisonment, albeit in a golden cage. Black lacquered bars topped by brass balls are really only pleasing to the human eye and are not things that horses really care about.

For many horses their daily life is characterised by excessively luxurious surroundings, anthropomorphism in the way they are handled, with hardly any social contact with other horses and little freedom of movement. If you look into the eyes of our apparently well looked-after European horses you will often discover a deep sadness. If we claim to be really animal friendly then we should at least be prepared to engage with our animals! And not just from on high, governed by time pressures, ambition and pride and often armed to the back teeth.

Unfortunately horses have no cry of pain. In the wild any noise might attract the attention of predators. This is why horses speak with their bodies. This goes on constantly as there is, after all, always something to say. It is unfortunate though that only very few people really look out for and are able to interpret correctly the signals constantly being given out by horses.

My job consists primarily of watching and understanding. Only then can I predict what a horse is going to do next and capture precisely THAT perfect moment, without having to rely on the motor drive of a high-tech camera to rattle off a sequence of shots."

The basics – the ABC of the equine language

Evolution has significantly shaped the horse's character and thus also the way these animals communicate. Even our domesticated horses are still herd animals as well as animals of flight. Here I will try to briefly touch on what this means for the life of a horse. If it is something you are particularly interested in there are some really good books that deal more with equine behaviour than with equine language. Since both are naturally closely connected with each other, behaviour will be mentioned briefly here before I move on to look more closely at the way horses express themselves.

Life in the herd

As an animal that has been developed to live in a herd, a horse needs and looks for other horses as constant companions in order to feel safe and secure. Typical of herbivores, it is also an animal of flight that ensures its survival mainly through heightened alertness and where necessary swift flight. Within any herd there are – as in every social community – certain structures and rules that have to be followed and obeyed otherwise chaos would break out and anarchy would rule. Disorganisation within a herd would be particularly dangerous if a predator were to attack it in the wild: organised flight would then be impossible as it would not be clear which member of the herd the rest should be following. Even for today's domesticated horses an ambiguous herd structure poses certain dangers. If the leader of a herd is suddenly removed, from one day to the next (for example if its owner moves yards), then the remaining members of the herd have to sort things out amongst themselves and work out who the new herd leader will be. While this happens serious injuries can occur since this "sorting out" will rarely occur without a certain amount of kicking and biting – unless of course it is clear to all who number two is from the start.

Its herd is essential for the survival of any horse. It offers protection, security and support and enables it to evolve and develop freely.

Even in homogeneous herds arguments can break out from time to time.
Usually though the tussles occur without real injury to anyone.

Hierarchy

The all-powerful herd stallion that, it was assumed for decades, took lead position within the herd structure has never really existed in the horse world. Wide-ranging observations and research have resulted in the conclusion that although there is no doubt that a hierarchy exists within any herd, this hierarchy is not absolute or unalterable. Horses too can have different jobs that are assigned to them for just a certain period of time. To be clear, I am referring in this instance to domesticated horses and not to horses in the wild – most horse owners are unlikely to have any contact with these.

In my own herd I am able to observe specific allocation of responsibilities and roles: the group clown, the minder who watches over the herd while the others rest and who is also the first to signal danger by suddenly raising its head or jumping to the side and finally the boss who is the first to tell newcomers who has the final word. Once the newcomer has started to settle in and begins to be integrated into the herd then lower-ranked horses will start to put it in its place while the herd leader will be more tolerant. There will often be much more violent disputes between lower-ranked members of the herd and newcomers than between the leader and the newcomer. This is because their ranking within the herd is much more at risk due to the horses being similarly assertive. New horses will work themselves up through the herd's hierarchy from the bottom to the top. Geldings that have a high opinion of themselves will have a harder time of it as they will automatically demand a higher position from the start. They can't or won't accept a lower position and will always question the hierarchy, which can lead to unrest in the herd. A new mare tends to be monopolised by the herd leader and will often become his new favourite. In relation to the lower-ranked geldings the mare will then find things much easier since the geldings will unquestioningly accept the leader's claim of ownership. Between the older and newer mares in the herd however fierce battles can break out and these are often more dangerous that those between the males.

When adolescent Haflingers come together there is never a quiet hoof.
They will play together, lock horns with one another and generally train for adulthood.

Change of power

An individual's ranking can change within an existing herd. One of my Spanish horses was the boss in his group for many years. When he first joined the group (at that stage there were only two Fjord mares and three Shetland geldings) within ten minutes he had already mounted the girls and chased the boys away across the paddock. Thus it was crystal clear who the boss was – until over the years larger geldings joined the group. Then it got very stressful. The Spaniard would often bully the herd in daily life, flexing his muscles and demonstrating his power by moving them all quite unnecessarily from one place to another without apparent reason. Valeroso was not a confident leader and had to prove constantly to the others who had the main say. He sustained an injury that meant he had to be removed from the herd for three months and kept by himself in a pen, which gave the Fjord gelding Eric the opportunity to seize control. And so it remained even

when Valeroso returned to the herd. Since then everything has become much more settled. As a more phlegmatic type, Eric has no need to prove his strength by constantly chasing the herd about. It is more important for him to be the first one into the field, the first to the feed and the mineral lick and the first to drink. Apart from this he is very tolerant. And Valeroso has also become much more relaxed since then. Eric isn't above playing with the Shetlands without getting aggressive – very different from Valeroso back then.

Finally when my Konik mare had a foal and she, together with my Fjord mare, Mali (who until then had clearly stood beneath Eric in the herd and allowed herself to be ordered about at will), were jointly responsible for looking after and protecting the filly, this marked the end of Eric's rule. Although he was still boss for the rest of the herd, the female trio had Eric well under control and it was the "boss" that had to get out of their way.

Changes of role and ranking like this occur again and again in herds, regardless of whether it is a fixed group of horses with few newcomers or a herd in a yard that sees new members join it on a monthly basis. In the latter though there is often less trouble, despite the frequent changes, since there is never any real opportunity for a fixed herd structure to develop and there is more of a sense of acceptance of, and even resignation to, the constant change.

There can also be less disruption when groups are divided on the basis of gender. For this reason many livery yard owners will consciously separate mares and geldings into separate herds. This avoids the disputes between geldings over a mare and vice versa. Many mare owners also don't like it when a gelding tries to mount their mare as it can be dangerous when the horses are shod or when the gelding is too large or heavy for the mare.

Mares and geldings show different social behaviours and play differently together. While geldings will often instigate chasing and fighting games with each other that can often get quite violent, mares usually prefer mutual grooming – it's all much more civilised.

By separating the genders the sexual and reproductive elements are taken out of the mix which leads to less tension (but also to more monotony, which I see in my own mixed herd with all its flirtations). Without wanting to be disparaging, it is possible to see a lot of the way people treat one another reflected in a herd. It is all about distribution of resources. The more limited the resources are – such as feed, water, sex/reproduction, the best shelter from the rain or sun and even the attention and affection from the two-legged service personnel – the greater the fight for them.

Emotions

For horses living in a herd, emotions play an important role. They have feelings such as fear, hunger, tiredness and pain as well as joy, reluctance, grief, uncertainty and affection. Competitive feelings between horses also play an important role, whether you call it envy or jealousy. This can also occur in relation to the two-legged animal in the herd. The closer the connection an animal has to "his" human, the more it will, depending on the type of horse, watch out for who gets what attention. And when the coveted person turns away the frustration will be taken out on its rival – by driving it away by either biting or kicking. Such expressions of emotion can be observed especially when you have a close relationship with a number of horses. The owner of one horse is unlikely to experience this type of behaviour since he or she will always be number one and is likely to only have to look after this one animal.

Sometimes however even just helping a friend out with his or her horse can lead to these petty jealousies emerging. When the horse returns to the herd your own may well take out its feelings on your friend's horse.

In most cases jealous behaviour has more to do with the apportionment of treats, which often accompany any activity involving horses, rather than with the attention given. In other words it is matter of resources, i.e. feed, rather than attention.

Life within a herd consists of many different components that are intertwined rather than it being a rigid structure. There are firm friendships, but also bitter feuds. For this reason it is important to discover whether your own horse has found friends in its own herd or whether it is a loner, constantly standing alone. In my own herd it has sometimes taken up to a year before a pony has really become integrated into the herd rather than just being tolerated. This is something that those people who constantly change yards at the drop of a hat should really think about. Loneliness and isolation can make our four-legged friends just as sad and unwell as they do us.

We aren't just responsible for schooling and training our horses properly, but also for ensuring that for the 22 or 23 hours of the day that we aren't there, our horses are well and that their requirements for social interaction, movement and appropriate feed are satisfied.

Birds of a feather ...

The mare on the left is indicating curiosity and friendly interest with her pricked ears. The mare on the right is showing defensive behaviour with her laid-back ears and half-hearted snapping. Her eyes however indicate her inferiority and that she is feeling unsure.

Misunderstandings

As a human how can I recognise these expressions of emotion and identify the individual positioning of a horse within the hierarchy of a herd? First and foremost I can achieve this through observation. Many breeds of horses even have their own "dialects" which can lead to misunderstandings between horses themselves. In a herd comprising solely of Icelandic horses, different ways of expression are used compared with a herd of warmbloods or Arabians. The physical differences between the breeds can in particular lead to clear differences in the way they express themselves. The longer head of a warmblood with its larger mouth opening will appear rather more threatening than a cute pony pulling the same face, even if both mean exactly the same thing.

Horses have to learn this language themselves. For this reason it is important that they grow up within a herd which offers lots of opportunities for communication with a wide range of other horses, rather than just growing up with their mother in a field behind the house. Foals raised in such isolation can have real problems relating to other horses later on since they only know their "mother" tongue and are also usually rather spoilt by their mother. No boundaries will have been drawn and they will find these hard to accept when set by you. You should therefore always find out, wherever possible, how exactly any new four-legged partner of yours has been raised and kept before you get it.

Body language comprises up to 90 per cent of a horse's language and these signals can be graded into different levels. Just as with the letters of the alphabet we have to learn to observe the different parts of our horses' bodies to understand what they are saying. An expression or phrase can only really be understood when seen and read in context. The "letters" of a horse's alphabet are its ears, eyes, muzzle, the tension through its body, the way it hold its tail, how it positions its legs and the way it positions its body in relation to the opposing horse or person.

In the following section of this book a number of different forms of expression will be introduced and then put into an appropriate context so that they can be interpreted.

> ## Observation – the key to understanding
> There are no shortcuts to learning the language of your horse: you have to watch them carefully in all types of situations! The time that you invest in this is paid back a hundredfold as it will enable you to identify problems at an early stage whether when handling or riding your horse, or in identifying when your horse isn't well.

The many faces of the horse

Anyone who knows their horse well and has taken time to observe it carefully can with one glance at its face tell you how it is feeling. Just as with people, the face expresses a huge range of emotions, from tiredness, joy, humour, pain and fear through to insecurity.
A second glance then at the tail, positioning of the legs and muscle tone are all just a confirmation of what the face has already told us.

The ears

For laymen or people beginning their journey with horses the position of the ears is supposedly the easiest way of identifying a horse's mood: ears pricked forwards – everything is alright; ears pinned back – danger. Fortunately it isn't as easy as this as if it were we would miss out on an unbelievably wide range of nuances.
Of course ears that are pinned back indicate that the horse is preparing to be aggressive. However, to what extent danger really exists will depend on what other signals are being given and the situation the horse finds itself in. In some cases ears that are laid back are just a threat. In other cases it is the build-up to a physical attack that immediately follows. Anyone who can't differentiate the two is living dangerously ... both as horse and human.
Similar misunderstandings can also occur when the ears are pricked attentively forwards. For us this is usually a positive expression, since horses really do look very "cute" like this. If the horse's attention though is focused on something a long way away from you then it can be dangerous as it will pay no attention to the two-legged companion standing next to it. I will tell you more about this in the chapter "Communicating with people".
It is also significant for the horse's mood whether the ear is turned to the side, to the ground or behind it.

The attentive but unexcited positioning of the ears shows this horse's divided attention: there is something of interest both in front of it as well as to its right.

The ears here have been put in the "switched off" position and the entire expression is that of a dozing, relaxed horse that feels safe and therefore doesn't need to use its ears to pay attention to its surroundings.

This clearly shows the ears giving out aggressive signals, the horse ready to attack at any moment and accompanied by a tossing of the head, which is indicated by the way the mane is moving.

This is an attentive face with pricked ears in an exciting but not alarming situation.

The most typical sign shown by a horse's nostrils: the flehmen response. Many, but not exclusively, male animals attempt to better pick up interesting smells by doing this.

Extremely flared nostrils which are typical for some breeds after even a minimum of physical exertion. The mouth and eyes are relaxed.

The nostrils

Even the shape of the nostrils that a horse is born with can determine a horse's natural expression. Arab horses often have very large, wide nostrils which they flare even wider at the slightest provocation. This naturally gives them a very hot-blooded, temperamental expression. The same type of nostrils in the case of a pony can have an even more dramatic effect.

The colder a horse's native country of origin is, then as a rule the smaller the nostrils are since these act as a way of the horse regulating its own temperature. Under normal circumstances a horse will breathe through its nostrils as well of course as using them to smell. In addition to this they are also a fantastic indicator of a horse's feelings. If a horse feels pain, is unwell or is becoming antagonistic it is able to wrinkle up its nostrils. The horse can also tense them and make them smaller in cases of disagreement and also when feeling strained, and, as already mentioned, the nostrils can be flared wide open when the animal is excited or aroused.

The flehmen response is a further special characteristic which, by pulling back the upper lip, allows access to the Jacobson or vomeronasal organ. By doing this the horse is better able to detect and interpret scents, particularly sexual ones (pheromones). Here we therefore already have a combination of nostrils and mouth speaking together.

The muzzle

For me the muzzle is one of the most fascinating parts of a horse's body. And it's not just me, if you look at the reaction of many people when they meet a horse. Most of them will put their hand out and try to stroke the horse's muzzle. It is one of the most expressive parts of a horse's body since there are many muscles located in and around it which allow the horse to use its mouth and change its expression.

The mouth is used to eat and drink and the lips and tongue, in conjunction with the sense of smell and taste, are able to distinguish exactly what is and is not edible. The mouth is also used to "feel" and check out unfamiliar objects, to pamper best friends by mutual grooming and nibbling as well as giving a thorough licking. Mutual touching and nibbling around the mouth often leads to friendly play. The area around the mouth can show relaxation and tension as well as anticipation, for example when the top lip is extended in expectation of receiving something really tasty. The mouth can also be used to carry objects (such as when stealing the manure skip) and to open doors.

And of course the mouth can also bite. It is most comparable to the human hand.

> **Grazing muzzle – yes or no?**
> For a horse the muzzle is an immensely important part of its body and it has a much greater role than just being used to take in feed. For this reason I think it more than questionable when a horse is made to wear a grazing muzzle 24 hours a day within a herd to restrict its grass intake. It also restricts its ability to interact with its companions! I would instead recommend a more complex pasture management, in which the individual requirements of each of the horses are taken into consideration.

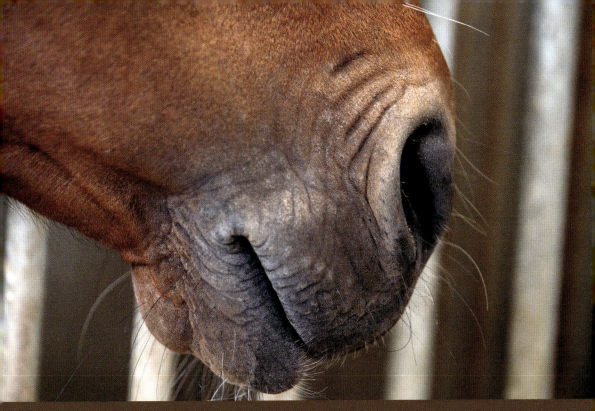

This is a typical example of mouth and nostrils that express not only discontentment and displeasure but also the beginnings of aggression – dependent on the other signals being given out.

This Shire horse shows a high level of relaxation with a totally floppy bottom lip.

If, when out in the field, my horses allow me to softly stroke them around their mouth, allowing me to run my fingers along the lips (and even possibly giving them a gentle kiss) then this is a sign of trust and affection as they will only allow this when truly relaxed. Horses themselves will also touch each other and gently nibble one another carefully. Not every horse however likes to be touched in this way and you just have to accept this.

Nibbling around the mouth is usually the precursor of an extensive period of play which depending on what the ground is like can end in a frantic game of chase. In winter when it is muddy and the rain appears to be never-ending then often the horses will leave it at gently biting each other although what starts gently can, in the heat of the moment, lead to more serious injuries. What might start as a nibble can end in a real bite and blood flowing.

My Fjord mare, Mali, has one of the most active mouths that I have ever encountered. It is never still and is always involved in some form of twitching, trembling or quivering and yet she is one of those horses that dislikes being touched around the mouth. Until now no one has been able to give me any idea of whether there is a connection at all.

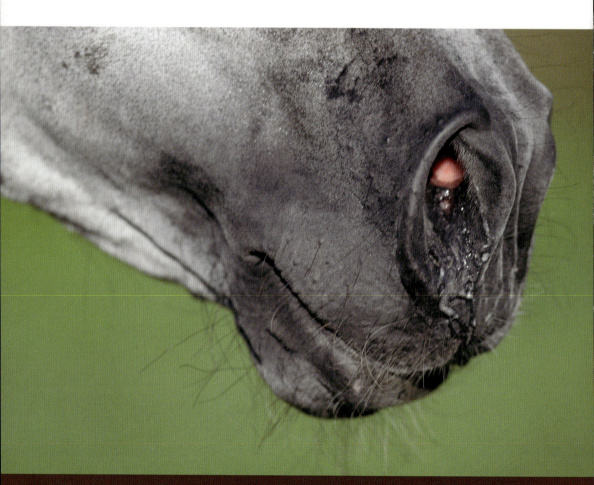

The opposite is the case with this Iberian horse. It is showing all the signs of tension: lips pressed together, tension around the mouth and nostrils and sucked-in cheeks.

The grey looks relaxed but interested. The nostrils are flared in an attempt to get more information about the smell it has picked up.

It is lovely when a horse can look into the world through such calm contented eyes.

The eyes

Eyes don't play a large role in communication between horses as at a distance they obviously can't see each other's eyes, they do however play a large role for us if we want to find out what sort of mood a horse is in.

The eyes are the mirror of the soul – for horses just as much as they are for us. You will often hear advice telling you not to look a horse straight in the eye as it will feel threatened. In my opinion, it is how you look at it that is significant.

Eye contact
I have often observed that my ponies will actively try to catch and hold my eye as if we were to look deep into each other's souls and ascertain how each other was feeling.
I can tell my horses off when they are out in the field just by giving them a certain look but can equally calm them down with a different one. This is particularly useful when I am teaching someone who is inexperienced or insecure in the saddle, which in turn can make the pony itself uncertain. One look from me, sometimes a warning, at other times an encouragement as if to say "you can do it" works perfectly. One of my cheekier ponies, Lasse, actually seems to try and catch my eye just before he is planning to take off in canter as this then allows him to be prevented from doing so by a stern look from me.

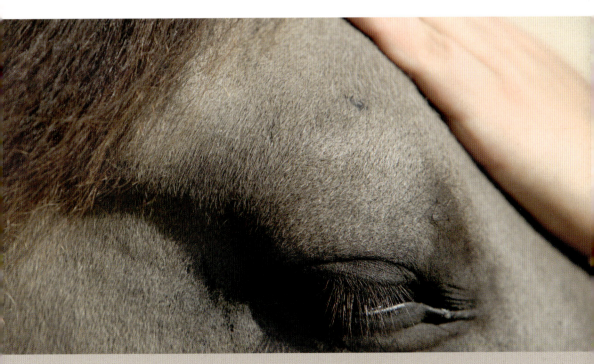

This is what a relaxed eye looks like. This Konik obviously enjoys being touched by "his" person. You can see the same expression when a horse is dozing.

Tired, sad, resigned: an expression that can often be seen in Iberian horses and in over-competed sports horses. Wrinkles around the eyes, particularly amongst young horses, are always a sign of emotional and/or physical stress and strain.

Fear has caused this horse to open its eyes so wide that you can see the whites of its eyes as it tries to look behind it to check that it is safe.

A horse obviously also needs its eyes to see. As an animal of flight this sense is fundamental for its existence. Blind horses have been able to survive in a herd and avoid being rejected from it thanks mainly to the help and lead given by good friends. Blind horses regularly prove themselves under saddle by performing to the highest levels. Amongst others, Bent Branderup and his famous – and blind – Knabstrupper stallions prove this point.

Due to the positioning of the eyes on the side of the head, horses have a very different angle of vision from us. This gives them an almost 360-degree field of vision. It is only immediately in front of and behind them that they can't see anything without turning their heads.

Since a horse doesn't have eyebrows it does make it slightly more difficult for us to interpret their expression – but not impossible. The shape and form the eye takes can tell us a lot – wide open or shut, how much white can be seen, how many wrinkles appear above the eye or the very expressive hollows over the eyes. All of these give us information about our horse's state of mind.

The body

Just as we do, the horse also can show how it is feeling through its body and the way it carries itself and moves. The slumped shoulders of a person equate to a horse's drooping neck – whether from tiredness, boredom, illness or resignation. Which of these is the case is decided by the eyes, ears, facial expression and the positioning of the legs. The muscle tone (the state of tension or tonicity of a muscle) is what is responsible for the way the horse carries itself – beginning with the nostril, up to the ears, the raised or lowered neck, tensed stomach muscles or the sunken back along to the raised or clamped-down tail. Horses that are very tense appear almost to stand on the tips of their hooves – even more than they already do. The muscle groups that run along a horse's top line from the top of the neck behind the head to the base of the tail are all connected, which is why you will never see a horse put its tail up in excitement when it has a relaxed and lowered neck.

It looks beautiful – but would be hard for someone to deal with in this state of excitement.

All three Icelandic horses are in exactly the same place but react very differently. Whilst the horse on the right looks very tense with its raised head and upright neck, the horse on the far left is just showing a degree of interest without being as tense through its body. The third horse in the group isn't letting its eating be interrupted.

Dangerously good-looking

The image of a horse with an upright neck and head, ears pricked forward, flared nostrils, tensed muscles and a tail carried high are for many the epitome of power, beauty and spirit. Quite rightly this is an eye-catching image whether on a photo or in a field. Many of us would love a poster of our favourite horse pictured like this hanging on our wall at home. But on a day-to-day basis when dealing with horses, this type of body language is a sign of impending danger and not of well-being, trust and relaxation.

Head position

As an animal of flight, horses react extremely sensitively to any alteration in their fellow herd members' silhouette. They use this to communicate with each other over long distances. Just lifting the head when grazing says to the other members of the herd, "just a minute, something is up!". Whether it just remains a matter of lifting the head or whether the horses then take flight will depend on whether what caused the first horse's attention to be caught is judged as being strange and threatening or as something that is familiar and trusted.

Learning to trust from others
A good example of this comes from my Konik mare, Baschka. She is a rescue case and until she came to us had had little contact with people, living instead in a herd in Mecklenburg-Vorpommern. Not long after she had come to us and been integrated into my herd I walked out into the

A good example of an allocation of duties. While part of the herd rests and lies down another member of the herd stands on watch.

field and approached the herd. Baschka immediately raised her head with wide eyes and flared nostrils. Her entire body and posture showed that she was ready for flight. As none of the other ponies however showed any indication whatsoever of lifting their heads long enough to leave the lush grass they were grazing on she noticeably relaxed and after a short time began to graze again. Looking at the behaviour of her fellow herd members was enough to calm her. Today she doesn't even bother raising her head when I go out into the field – a shame really ...

Depending on how safe a horse feels in its herd, it will tend to react more or less to unfamiliar outside influences. The reaction shown will greatly depend on the temperament of the individual. For this reason when buying a new horse you should always try to observe it in its own herd beforehand. How confident is it with the others, how does it react to outside influences, how quickly does it get wound up and how long does it then take to settle down again?

Fear can be catching!
Recently Baschka's foal, Grazina, was playing with a blue rubbish bag that had somehow landed in the field. She picked it up in her mouth and frightened herself so much by the sound of its rustling that she ran away – unfortunately with the bag still clamped firmly between her teeth so that it floated alongside scaring her even more. My 18-head herd that is usually so laid back had never seen anything like it before and took off on their own mini-stampede as the rubbish bag approached them. After three circuits Grazina finally opened her mouth and the scary episode came to an end. Whilst my more self-assured ponies settled back down immediately into their usual routine, the more nervous-minded were still wound-up 30 minutes later and remained very suspicious of any sound or movement.

In such a frightening situation as this a horse's immediate reaction is to run away first and then look at what caused the scare. The herd instinct escalates the situation since the first one to react is quickly joined by the rest. In the case of minor "disturbances" a horse will raise its head, look, turn its head in case the other eye can see something that the first one can't, prick its ears and rotate them, glance at its friend and then usually relax again.

If the horses are out as a herd either full time or for many hours at a time then during periods of grazing (up to 16 hours a day) there will be times of rest. In these rest phases individual animals will be selected to watch over the rest of the herd while they lie down to sleep or doze standing up. In familiar surroundings it is usually the lower-ranked horses that act as guards since the head of the herd has to gather its strength for more important things. However they too must get the opportunity to lie down for a rest. For this reason it is important to give horses that are not totally accepted into the herd a chance to rest without being threatened by the others by giving them a separate paddock or stable at least overnight to have a break from the herd.

When you see an entire herd at rest lying down then you can assume from this that they feel very safe and secure in their surroundings.

For us, a horse with a very alert stance should always be a sign that it should be handled with particular care and attention. If the relationship between human and horse isn't so well established that the person is the herd leader who imparts trust and confidence then you are at risk of being trampled if, as a result of the horse's tension and watchfulness, it prefers to take flight over trusting you. If a horse can't be settled or calmed down by a person then that person has little influence and is therefore not in charge.

The neck

When a horse lifts its head it doesn't always indicate danger to the other members of the herd. This will depend on the angle of the neck, i.e. how high the head is lifted, whether the neck is tensed and if the horse tries, by turning the head quickly back and forth, to better assess the situation. If one of the horses on watch shows this type of behaviour then it is unlikely that any of the rest will remain calmly lying down.

A head that is held high with a tensed neck showing every muscle strand is also an indication of authority and a possible power struggle. This happens naturally more commonly in the case of male animals than with females. There is more about this in the chapter on "Patterns of behaviour between horses".

In the same way that excitement is expressed by a horse lifting its head and neck, so too can relaxation, trust and exhaustion be reflected through head and neck. A horse that drops its head and neck has given away control – whether it be out of a sense of trust, exhaustion, pain or just resignation. You have to very carefully observe and put the action into the right context in order to be able to recognise the differences. And here too the same thing applies as before:

A small group of Icelandic horses dozing with their heads lowered and relaxed expressions.

the more carefully you can observe your horse in a variety of everyday situations then the faster you will be able to tell what its state of mind and physical condition is.

When a horse is standing with its head lowered it makes a real difference knowing whether it is a horse dozing and relaxing in the sun after grazing, whether it is standing in its stable or in the field totally exhausted after a hard training session, whether on health grounds it is totally listless and barely has enough strength to lift its head or whether a horse is so inwardly resigned because any joy in its life and all of its strength has been beaten or starved out of it. Sometimes even just a "normal" life as a misunderstood leisure-partner or piece of "sports equipment" is enough to make a horse give up inside. What is sensible and comfortable for us isn't always in the best interests of our horses.

The position of the neck is a real give-away in identifying when there is a relaxed and contented relationship with humans – whether from the ground or when being ridden. In addition the neck plays a great role in a dominant stallion or gelding expressing its position over its mares and the rest of the herd – and sometimes towards humans as well when the hierarchy hasn't really been established. More on this in the chapter dealing with "Communication with people".

There is something exciting going on: expressions are tense, with wide-open eyes, pricked ears, raised heads with tensed under-neck muscles, lips pressed tightly together and, in the case of the foal, you can see signs of chewing.

As tight as a bow string: this horse is using its neck to gather enough energy for a really good buck.

Its tail lifted and waved like a flag – so typical of Arab horses and several other breeds this clearly expresses the inner tension of these easily excitable horses.

The tail

As mentioned earlier, a horse's individual muscle groups are all connected from the front to the back. Depending on the breed of horse and thanks to the muscles in its dock the tail can be held in a variety of angles to the body depending on the degree of excitement. This is best seen in Arab horses when they wave their tail about like a flag, so typical of the breed. Sometimes the aid to canter is enough to result in this tail position. The tail is a wonderful indicator of a horse's state of tension – or lack thereof – both physical and mental.

As well as being a mode of communication the dock, when well covered with hair, also of-fers protection against the elements for the sensitive parts of the body located between the horse's buttocks. For this reason you should never pull a horse's tail when it is going to be turned out into the wind and rain.

As well as indicating the level of excitement by the angle at which the tail is held – whether out of fear, danger or as an expression of dominance or to impress the other members of the herd by making itself look bigger – the tail is primarily used as a defence against flies and other insects.

As soon as the weather gets bad, horses will turn their well-upholstered rumps to the wind.

You can compare it to someone nervously tapping their fingers repeatedly on the table. Horses that constantly switch their tails back and forth – without flies being the reason – are in the second phase of issuing a threat. Usually this is preceded by another clearly threatening expression, often the ears being laid back. If that doesn't suffice, then the tail starts to switch. When even that isn't enough then the legs start to issue signals as well. And when even this isn't paid attention to and appropriately reacted to then a bite or kick should be no big surprise.

A sudden swish of the tail as an expression of discontent more often than not has something to do with physical pain or discomfort. It is an indication of not liking being touched in a particular place, whether the touch comes from another horse or a person, and can also be shown as a symptom of painful conditions such as colic, laminitis and similar. Unfortunately you often see this too in ridden horses when there is obvious and often painful tension in the horse. It can however also mirror a horse's internal state of tension or excitement usually when a horse notices that it is in a situation that it can't get away from by flight, such as when tied up, in stocks or when it is cornered. To the same extent a loosely swinging relaxed tail is a sign of relaxedness and suppleness. Something which is especially significant in Icelandic horse equitation is the tail's so-called tolt-wave.

Well-respected trainers and veterinarians can recognise by the position that the tail is held in – often crookedly instead of being held straight – where the causes of tension and difficulties in riding lie. Sometimes these are inborn but in the majority of cases they have been "ridden in".

And of course the way a mare in season holds her tail is an indication of when she is ready to be covered.

An example of mares exchanging blows with the ladies standing rear-to-rear and having a go at each other, accompanied by much squealing. It usually sounds worse than it actually is.

Leg signals

There are a number of different positions that a horse's legs can take up that have nothing to do with either movement or feeding but everything to do with communication. A horse resting one of its back legs with just the toe of one hoof touching the ground can be a sign of relaxation when the horse is dozing, but it can also be a sign of pain. A slightly raised back hoof can just as easily be a threat and here too it is important to look at the interaction of the individual parts of the body in order to best interpret the signs.

A horse can rest one of its back legs without actively engaging any of its muscles in the hindquarters and this is recognised by the leg being bent. The patellar ligaments which run from the patellar to the fibula in the stifle joint can be hooked over the patella and "fix" the stifle in extension. This means that the horse can stand with little muscular effort while the other leg can be relaxed with the tip of the toe just touching the ground.

The most expressive way for a horse to use its legs is probably to kick out with its hind legs. I hope that you have never been the target of such an attack. Horses that intentionally kick out at people must either be under a lot of pressure or feel very greatly threatened for them to resort to such serious measures against a person. Alternatively they may have had such bad experiences with people that they prefer to keep them at a distance by kicking.

Healthy legs are essential for a horse's survival. Broken legs or injuries to the limbs could mean death. In normal day-to-day life kicks usually meet thin air or a well-upholstered bottom rather than a more vulnerable leg.

A typical example of a herd relaxing together. Some of them are lying down, some are standing quietly with their ears turned back, indicating in this case that they are relaxed. The skewbald and the fjord horse are resting a hind leg which takes some of the strain off their muscles.
(Photo: Daniela Bolze)

Hard-hitting dwarf
A yard owner wanted to muck out in a hurry so put one of his horses together with a Shetland pony in a large stable just while he quickly did the job. Both of the animals knew each other from grazing out together. In the restricted space though with little opportunity to get away a hefty attack took place – from which the Shetland came out the winner. Thanks to its shorter legs, rather than hitting the horse's well-muscled and thus protected hindquarters it managed to come into contact with its much more vulnerable legs. As a result of this the horse was unable to be ridden for the rest of its life!

More often than not you see a kick being threatened by the hindquarters rather than it actually being carried out since in most cases this has been preceded by the ears being laid back, the tail being swished and a clear warning movement of the horse's head.

Another important leg movement is the striking out of the front leg – typical display behaviour of stallions. Mares too though, when meeting a horse for the first time, will often react by stamping or striking out with a front foot usually following a squeal. Should you not step in to prevent it, mares will often then turn their quarters round to each other to have a go with their hind legs. Male horses prefer rearing and biting as the next step.

Horses also like to use their forelegs as hand-replacements to investigate objects, open gates or to move water buckets, rails or indeed anything else that happens to be lying around. This can extend to playing football with their beloved horseball. They also come in handy for scraping soil away from roots or to separate out the old hay from the really tasty stuff that is right at the bottom of the pile.

Your imagination needs no bounds when it comes to the uses to which a horse's forelegs can be put. When a horse though stretches its forelegs far out in front whilst tucking its hind legs well underneath it then call your veterinarian immediately! This is usually a sign of a severe case of either laminitis or colic with the horse trying to gain a little relief from the pain.

The pain can't be shown any more clearly: a horse that is standing with its legs stretched out in front like this is usually trying to gain some relief from the pain of laminitis in its front feet.

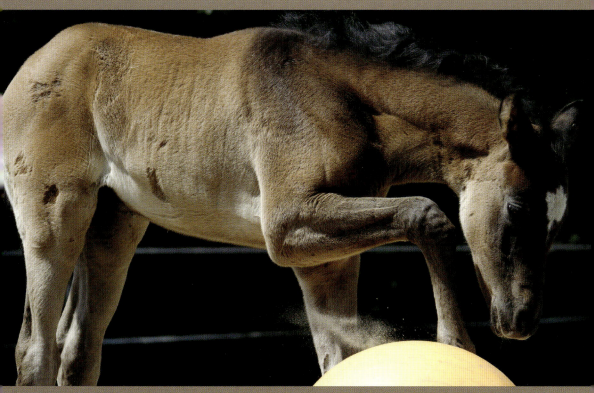

Foals like investigating new things with their front legs.

Interpreting vocalisations correctly

As animals of flight horses have a very limited repertoire of vocal sounds since these would give them away to their attackers. Despite this they do have several sounds that they use to make themselves understood with the herd.

Whicker

The most beautiful sound for me is the deep and almost tender whicker that a mare makes to her foal or that two horses that have a close relationship will greet each other with. It's a bit like a deep, gentle mumbling sound at frequent but differing length intervals, almost like: Mh-mh-mh-mh. The volume will vary depending on the situation and the horse. It is almost like a neigh but with the lips closed.

With a lot of luck and on good days my own horses will greet me like this as well – it is a sound that makes all the hard work and effort that are involved in looking after the horses worth it for at least that day.

You will frequently hear a horse whicker when feed is involved. If the feed arrives quickly and there is no stress then you will only hear an expectant whicker. The more a horse feels stressed, is greedy or wants its feed faster the more insistent and vehement the noises made will become, up to a penetrating whinny often emphasised by impatient kicking at the stable door. You will often experience this type of behaviour in large livery yards where the made-up feeds are taken around on a large trolley from stable to stable when the horses are standing in. In situations like this you will also often see horses acting aggressively towards their neighbours since the horses are obviously worried that they won't get their share of feed and so are ready to fight for it.

Defining moments
The whicker is the sound which a mare uses to imprint herself on her foal. I have been privileged to experience this twice in my own herd. When Grazina, my Konik foal, was born, my Fjord mare, Mali, paid so much attention to her and looked after her so much that the foal actually tried to suckle from her and thought Mali was her mother – especially as both mares, Mali and Grazina's mother, were the same colour. With a heavy heart I had to separate them and put Grazina and her real mother, Baschka, together by themselves for a few days so that they could build up a mother–daughter bond without Mali's interference.

Even after this though the trio remained inseparable and Mali is still a real surrogate mother for Grazina. Baschka too though is greeted by Mali with a gentle whicker when she is put back into the field – a sign of a deep bond.

A typical "neighing" expression with a slightly closed mouth through which the pony can call to its friend.

Neigh

The neigh is the most common call that horses use amongst themselves. It will always be used when horses can't communicate with each other as well, either because they are some distance apart or because something stands between them, such as a stable wall or a hedge, or because they have lost sight of one another, such as when they are at a competition. It is almost always a sign of anxiety or unrest – whether because a horse's best friend has left it (even when it is just for a short hack), or because it hasn't noticed that the rest of the herd has moved off to a different part of the field and it finds itself alone. The horse will whinny and then join the others as fast as it can.

If a horse is left out in a field while the others have been fetched in, it will almost always neigh to its friends. This is a situation that you should really avoid. As a herd animal a horse should never be left alone. Depending on the how insecure an animal feels, it can develop into a state of

hysteria. The result of this can be that it tries to jump out of the field or that it tries to pull away from the person leading it when it is finally fetched in. So many accidents could have been avoided if herd animals hadn't been thoughtlessly left alone. Anyone who has to deal with such an insecure horse will need sufficient authority and expertise to be able to give the horse enough of a feeling of security that it wants to stay with them.

When you do get back to the yard it is almost always the horses that have been left behind that whinny to the ones returning home, while the horses that are returning remain silent. This is a good sign for the rider–horse relationship as it shows that the rider has sufficient authority to ensure that the horse is concentrating on them and its work and that it isn't being led by its own instincts. Unfortunately you see this less often when it comes to those riding stallions that can't be controlled and that aren't really concentrating

Here the stallion is neighing in a challenging but not yet aggressive manner, with a wide-open mouth but no sign of teeth as yet.

on their riders. The horses bellow out around the arena in order to draw attention to themselves. This is the start of a ritual behaviour, in which an ever-increasing similar series of behaviours is shown, which in most cases is there for the purpose exclusively of impressing rivals and mares. This type of behaviour doesn't however belong anywhere near where there are people involved. A whinny is usually followed by the horse looking for the other horse, display behaviour in the form of the head and neck tensely stuck up in the air with the tension running through the horse's entire body from the tips of its ears to the lifted tail. If the handler or rider hasn't by this stage exerted their authority on the horse then they are in danger of just becoming a passenger.

A horse will almost always neigh when it sees or hears a strange horse. The neigh acts as an identification sound as we now know that horses are able to recognise each other through their voices.

If two stallions meet then the neighing can degenerate into real trumpeting with the mouth wide open but with the teeth remaining covered. This is quite different from the threatening call in which the teeth are bared. Stallions react just as loudly when an in-season mare approaches or moves away. Even when this challenging type of neighing is more a part of a stallion's repertoire, a similar ear-splitting battle cry will occur when mares fight, usually with the two opponents standing with their rears together and going hammer and tongs at each other. This may seem a very brutal scene but in reality is usually fairly harmless since their quarters are well-muscled. A horse's voice develops throughout its life when it comes to neighing. A foal's call for its mother sounds more like a high-pitched scream, whereas the mare's call, depending on her authority and the foal's age, will vary in volume. When a youngster is approximately two years old its voice will "break" and it will develop a deeper tone.

The pitch will also depend on a horse's emotional state. The more excited or frightened a horse is the higher the sound it makes will become until it becomes almost a cry of terror.

A fearful neigh with wide-open mouth and eyes.

Weapons on show

Behavioural researchers have discovered that the opening of the mouth to the side which occurs when horses, especially stallions, neigh when greeting or showing off to others served originally to reveal the stallion (canine) tooth and thus demonstrate its strength from the start to any rivals. A horse will primarily bite with its incisors: the canine teeth just reinforce its aggression.

Squealing

The high-pitched squeal is usually heard when there is a mare involved and mostly when two horses meet for the first time. Firstly they will lower their heads, sniff each other's noses and then almost always one or both will strike out with a foreleg at the same time as uttering a squeal. According to my own observations, it is usually the lower-ranked mare that squeals. Due to the likelihood of a foreleg striking out you should never stand too close to or between horses when they are greeting each other. If one of the ladies doesn't like the other then they could also turn round as fast as lightning and take a kick at the other. If a stallion approaches a mare that is in season and is a little too insistent then the mare will usually respond with a quiet, high-pitched squeal. If he remains pushy it can turn into more of a battle cry which you would think came from a pig rather than a horse. If you have a mixed herd you will hear sounds like this during the year when mares come into season and there are one or two geldings that are keen to try their luck.

Grunting and groaning

Here I am talking about noises that occur in all species – just like coughing and sneezing. You can hear horses grunting and groaning when in great pain, when giving birth, in falls or injuries or when horses are mating. Sometimes you will also hear these noises when horses are being ridden and are working hard or really concentrating. Unfortunately horses don't have different types of cries of pain, as for example a dog has when it whines or howls. If this were the case then it could get very loud in some yards and in certain manèges and arenas and we would have to fundamentally rethink a lot of what we inflict on our horses. Instead we have to learn the other signals that express pain and aversion.

Snorting and blowing

There are different gradations and ways of snorting. On the one hand there is the relaxed release of air through the nostrils when a tense situation proves to be harmless. This is most easily recognised when you are in the saddle and have warmed up your horse and it starts to relax. Horses will then gently give a deep and prolonged snort. This has the same effect on the body and mind of a horse as it does when you breathe deeply in and out. The ribcage lifts and falls and the stomach muscles tense and relax which has a direct effect on the back muscles.

But there is then the strongly accentuated, harder snort directed at strange objects or made when jumping. It has been suggested that in doing this, horses create a sound wave that allows them to better orientate themselves.

Whatever the case, to us, this short, hard snort means that the horse is very excited and is ready to take flight.

Stallions will give their own unique type of snort when they are really trying win over or show off to a mare.

Copy-cat effect
You can actually calm your horse and get it to tune into your own breathing rhythm by clearly and audibly breathing in and out and by using your lips to create a similar gentle snorting effect. This is why it is so important when handling horses or riding to pay attention to your own breathing technique and not forget to breathe.

An example of relaxed snorting when dozing or after activity.

Excited snorting in which the breath is blown out in bursts. It supposedly serves to help orientation.

Patterns of behaviour between horses

The behaviour of horses amongst themselves is of course dependent on whether they are in their normal day-to-day life or in an exceptional situation. Sometimes it is difficult for us to tell what an exceptional situation is and what is normal. Most of us have no idea how easy it is to confuse a horse just by interfering in its normal daily life or by putting new neighbours next to its field. For this reason I think it is very important to look more carefully at the day-to-day life of a horse in its herd.

Daily life in the herd

How much action and movement there is within a herd of horses depends entirely on the composition and structure of the herd. Currently the most common way of keeping horses is stabled, with full- or part-time turn-out in the summer and short or no turn-out in winter. Although this may be most convenient and practical for us, it doesn't mean that it is the best for our horses. There are other ways of keeping horses, including active and open turn-out, that better satisfy the needs of the horse for exercise and to live in a herd. These do however restrict the flexibility of the rider since integration within the herd takes longer and changing a yard is something that has to be carefully considered. In addition many horses that live out all year round get their exercise with their companions. When you get them in to ride they can appear rather less motivated that if they had been standing in a stable all day. On the other hand however many stabled horses can be difficult to handle since they can't fulfil their need for exercise and movement. This leads to bad behaviour when tied up, not standing still, pushing and rushing when being led. When ridden they will tend to buck as well. It is up to you to decide what is more important: a horse that is happy for 24 hours a day or one for which the rider is the highlight for an hour a day. And then in some circumstances the rider will have to put up with the horse letting off steam ...

Interactive turn-out

Lately active turn-out has become very fashionable in Germany. In this system the area that the horses have access to is divided up into sleeping, eating, drinking and resting zones which encourages the horses to move from one zone to the other to satisfy their basic needs and stay active. Automated feeding dispensers, which ensure that a constant supply of small quantities of feed is provided, are often used. In theory this method of keeping horses is very good. Whether this system works well though depends on the ability of the person running it to put the right horses together in the herd. The group mustn't be too large and the lowest-ranked member must be able to obtain sufficient feed.

When there is limited time given to grazing there is less likely to be time for games since eating will be given priority over everything else. But even in winter when there is no feed available you will often see bored-looking horses standing about when turned out.

Experience has shown me that the larger the horse, the less inclination to play it has. At home it is always the Shetlands that are responsible for any action – which can then encourage the big ones to join in. I have heard from others as well that horses that are larger than 15.3hh tend to be less playful than the smaller more mobile ponies or Iberian horses.

The tender nibbling around the mouth is an invitation to play.

The more the group comprises of a variety of ages, then the livelier it will tend to be. The youngsters play more amongst themselves as well as engaging the older, less active ones to join in more. Although the exception does prove the rule: there are of course many very agile older horses as well as lazy younger ones ... The gender mix in a herd will also play a great role. Geldings tend to engage more in play, particularly chasing and fighting games, while in herds consisting purely of mares it is all much more well-mannered with them more likely to engage other mares in mutual grooming. They often move out of walk only when being turned out into their field or when they are very young. Herds separated into mare and gelding groups tend to be more settled since there is no, or less, competition between the individual horses – by taking sex drive out of the equation you have removed the cause of so much tension but also the cause of much of the spirit and temperament in the horses. In mixed herds you will frequently find that some geldings will try to mount the mares. This sometimes results in injuries to the coat, skin and back, not to mention the issue of vaginal health. In my own case I keep mixed herds as I rarely have newcomers into the herd. I really enjoy seeing the ponies forming attachments with others. There are real couples that never leave each other's side unless absolutely necessary.

For a herd to enjoy real freedom of movement the ground conditions and the size of the turn-out or field are of key importance. No horse is going to enjoy moving about on a slippy, small muddy square of turn-out. The more unusual and elongated the turn-out area is, ideally with different types of surfaces and possibly with branches or tree trunks, the more horses are encouraged to move about. Turn-out is not all the same – as a horse owner you should always pay attention to what sort of turn-out your horse has access to.

An example of the knee-game, the aim being to nip the other in the foreleg.

A close friendship awake and asleep. These three are inseparable in virtually any situation.
(Photo: Daniela Bolze)

Friendships

It can take many months or even more than a year for ponies and horses to forge real friendships – sometimes they might even just not fit into the herd. Friendships can sometimes be life-long and as an owner you should very carefully consider whether you should separate horses just because you don't like something about the yard even though your horse may be settled and well looked after. The same applies if your horse doesn't settle in and remains isolated – in my opinion in this situation you should also look for another yard with new equine companions.

What is decisive for the forging of real equine affection, apart from the smell and genuine sympathy, can also be the coat colour and the age – but not necessarily. Experience has shown that more unusual colours such as greys or coloured horses find it harder to make friends, which is why particular attention should be paid to the composition of a herd and the need to ensure that there are several of these types. The breed can also be significant. Icelandic horses tend to be quite "racist" and can make it quite hard for new horses to become integrated into the herd.

Interestingly, in the case of my own herd, friendships tend to be more easily made between geldings and mares than between two mares. The ladies are very selective in their choice of close friends since obviously competition plays a role and they tend to like being accompanied by a firm male friend and enjoy mutual grooming with each other. In these friendships there is no sexual element but rather it is just a matter of having company. I have only ever seen one such close relationship between mares.

The smaller the ponies, the easier they find it often to settle into new herds. Could it be because of their size and perhaps not being taken so seriously and being seen as less aggressive? I don't know. In any case you would be wrong as it is often the little ones that torment the larger ones mercilessly and in the resulting fight usually come out on top because of their manoeuvrability.

Small but my, oh my! Here the smaller of the two is clearly the aggressor.

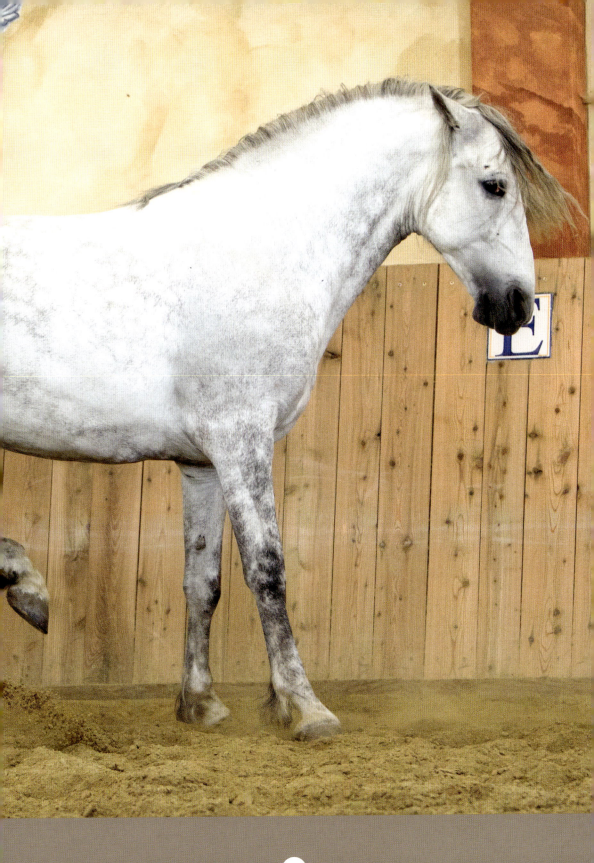

Only horses that like each other scratch each other like this – especially in the places that the horse can't easily reach themselves, the withers and the quarters.

Friendship carousel
Friendships can be very fluid. For many years our Shelty, Brownie, was in love with the Fjord mare, Mali. When Mali found true friendship with the Konik mare, Baschka, and only wanted to be with her, Brownie had to give way. He didn't *mourn for long though and instead attached himself immediately to the rather lovely Pretty and hasn't taken his eyes off her ever since. My geldings form friendships too, sometimes as threesomes.*

Usually lower-ranked ponies will attach themselves to a higher-ranked member of the herd and they clearly feel insecure and their position in the herd is weakened when the higher-ranked friend is taken in to be ridden and can no longer offer protection.

Nearly everyone will have heard a moving story about horses that have forged deep friendships and can't live without each other, through to the pony that won't leave the side of its blind friend as it acts as its eyes. Really closely befriended horses will almost never leave each other's sides. The will rest, eat and sleep next to one another. If possible they will even go to the trough and drink together. If you take one of the horses out of the field you will see how the other waits on its return. When its friend does return it will be met at the gate, greeted and then the two will go off together. Between such close friends you will also find that they engage in particularly intensive mutual grooming.

Daily routine and behaviour

A horse's daily routine is much more rigidly structured that most people imagine. Since I have the great fortune – and sometimes also the burden – of looking after, and thus being able to observe, my ponies all the time, I get to experience the varying phases that make up a horse's day. Typically a horse's daily routine is heavily influenced by us, depending on how long we turn them out for, and when we give them hard feed or want to work them.

Very early in the morning after the sun rises and before being fed, playtime takes over in the field. This usually involves the horses flattening all of the piles of droppings that are in the field and virtually "playing themselves warm".

After morning feeding, they will all drink and then rest for a while. When it comes to drinking there is a clear order, with the boss of the herd always being the first to drink and then the rest following in order of rank. The morning rest is usually quite short if the ponies are also being fed hay. Around 11 am there will be another play session although this one is usually not as wild as the early morning one. The colder the wind is, the more active the horses will be, if nothing else as a way of keeping warm. This is one of the reasons why it is important that horses have plenty of room to move around in. If the horses are out in the field in the morning they concentrate on eating with the occasional break for drinking. If they come in for the afternoon then they will have a lengthy rest – much longer than in the morning. Since I always have riding lessons from 3pm onwards the horses are forced into activity. On days when there are no lessons the horses will often chill out through until the late afternoon. They may move to a new spot in the field, depending on where the shade might move to. Only around 5 or 6pm will they start to play again. Horses that are stabled at night are usually in their boxes by this stage.

I always feed in the evenings around 7pm and then the herd will settle back down again for the night. It is only at dawn that the herd will start to wake up and become active again.

The phases of the day described here are not unique to my own herd, but have been observed by others in their own herds as well as by behavioural researchers. The individual phases of activity are of course determined to a certain extent by the routine of the individual yards. If you allowed horses their own choice then they would rest for up to nine hours a day. The remainder of the time would be spent grazing, playing or in mutual grooming.

Feeding

Feed envy plays an important role for horses. How well developed this tendency is will depend on how limited the feed is. In a large field with plenty of grass it is unlikely that this will be an issue. It is quite a different case though in a row of stables at feeding time. Ears will be laid back, neighbours will, to a greater or lesser degree, try to have a go at each other, the door will be banged by impatient forelegs and in some cases they may also try to take a piece out of the person doling out the feed.

In principle the highest-ranking animal has the right to be first to feed. In my herd I distribute the feed in six large tractor tyres. When I go out to fill them up the most dominant and strongest horses are at the front of the queue. The boss, Eric, will go to the first tyre with his closest friends while the rest have to wait until I have filled up the other tyres. Eric will then however go from tyre to tyre to check whether there is something tastier in any of the others. Every time he moves to a new tyre there is a domino effect as the ponies that he then drives away

move to a different tyre and in turn then drive the lower-ranked herd members and so on. It takes a while until they all settle down and can eat undisturbed. Only when the feed starts to run out do they start to move around again.

The hierarchy surrounding feeding makes it important that there are enough feeding stations for the lower-ranked animals to be able to move to. It is always best to have one more than there are animals since, as explained, horses do like to change stations. In any case a horse – regardless of rank – should always have access to feed without any danger of being injured or cornered.

Dangerous treats

If you always give your horses treats as a greeting, then you will find that the horses will always greet you with laid-back ears. This isn't a threat to you, but rather is meant as a warning and deterrent to the other herd members not to approach this precious source of food. In the heat of the moment however it can be dangerous for you too.

Grazing together as a herd on a lush field of grass is pure paradise for horses – especially when the sun is shining.

The laid-back ears indicate the initial signs of aggression focused on the tidbits that the woman is holding in her hands. This can quickly deteriorate into a real quarrel between the horses, ideally with the person not coming between them ...

Drinking

There are several phases involved in drinking. First of all you will observe a chewing motion or possibly the tongue being stretched out, probably to check the temperature and quality of the water. When drinking by opening the jaw with the lips closed horses create a vacuum in their mouth which helps them to slurp up the water – similar to us drinking through a straw. Horses can hold the water in their mouths in order to, amongst other things, bring it up to body temperature, which is something that I observed in my own Fjord mare, Hannah. She would hold the water in her mouth for a long time. If I offered her a treat at this stage without thinking about it, water would cascade out over my hand. When a horse is drinking you can see the sucking motion fantastically well by looking at its ears. Horses suck about five or six times before they swallow (this equates to about a litre of water). The process of drinking will often be interrupted by the horse lifting its head to check out the surrounding area, since watering holes were in prehistoric times where most predators would lie in wait. Even today this awareness of danger is still deeply rooted in our domesticated horses.

There is also a clear order and ranking when it comes to drinking.

Horses have very different individual needs when it comes to water, depending on the temperature, how active they are and the state of health of the individual animal. You should always ensure that any troughs or automatic water drinkers aren't too high for ponies to reach as low troughs are better suited to a horse's anatomy. A horse that isn't familiar with an automatic water drinker has to learn how to use one, either by putting it with other horses that know how to use one so that it can learn by watching, or by showing it how to use it yourself with your hand until it seizes the initiative itself. Sometimes it helps to put a piece of carrot in a half-full drinker to encourage the horse to put its muzzle into the bowl. At the first sounds of the water running in to fill it the horse is likely to pull back but will quickly get used to it. During this learning phase though you should still offer it water from a bucket so that it gets enough water until it has learnt to get it itself. Many horses love playing with water. If they have large

containers to drink from they will stick their heads right into the water, splash and blow into the water before beginning to drink. Apart from being playful this can also serve to check the water out.

Resting

A horse can rest standing up, half lying down resting on its chest or flat out on its side, depending on the weather and the ground conditions.

Thanks to the particular nature of their legs horses can relax and doze when standing up. As already described, thanks to the complicated structure of tendons and ligaments in the hind legs their muscles are able to rest totally. The structure is quite different for the forelegs. Here the triceps brachii have to stay tensed so that the forelegs don't collapse and fold up. For this reason horses have to lie down from time to time so that all their muscles have a chance to rest and recover.

This photo shows several resting positions: lying stretched out, half lying down with and without the muzzle supporting the head, standing with the leg bent and standing up properly.

There are also differing levels when it comes to lying down. These range from lying down with the legs underneath and head lifted up to the neck dropped down with the muzzle propping the head up (you can see real little nests in the straw when your horse does this) through to lying flat out with the legs stretched out. The latter will only happen when a horse really feels safe and well or when it is seriously ill and is suffering pain.

When dozing standing up or when half lying down horses will still be aware of external stimuli, recognised by the movement of their ears and tail. This is quite different from when they are in a deep sleep when, like us, you can see that they have entered a dream phase from their movements and noises. When sleeping, horses breathe deeply and regularly and may also moan and grunt, especially just before waking up. If you wake a horse up by touching it you can see how its breathing becomes shallower, its ears and eyes move before it lifts its head. Many people unfor-

tunately rarely experience their horse in a deep sleep since in most yards it is too hectic during the day and at night the yard is usually closed to visitors.

It takes a horse quite a bit of effort to lie down since it doesn't have a particularly mobile spine. It has to position its legs closer together underneath its body, which in itself involves so much effort that the muscles may start to quiver. Eventually it will bend the front legs before rolling to one side. For this reason, heavily in-foal mares will sometimes rather suddenly drop to one side and sick animals will sometimes just not lie down because of the effort involved especially when they have a leg injury.

To stand up, a horse will stretch out both forelegs in front of its chest, shoving its hind legs under itself and use its head and neck to create enough impulsion to get up on its forelegs and then with a jolt stand up onto its hind legs.

No sign of fear of the water here: by pawing the water with the foreleg the horse is checking out both the water and the ground conditions underneath before lying down. Some horses appear to love it when the water splashes up around them.

Rolling

Rolling – especially on sandy ground – is an important part of a horse's repertoire of behaviour. It has to be learnt as a foal and is often catching amongst herd-mates.

Horses roll to look after their coats which is why they prefer sandy conditions. Sandy soil sticks to a wet coat, absorbs the moisture and can later be got rid of by simply shaking. The result is that the horse will dry off more quickly. It is mainly moisture, whether it comes from sweating after being ridden, or playing, or from rain that really bothers horses. Parasites can also be another reason for frequent rolling.

Rolling is also often the conclusion of a relaxed phase of sunbathing. A horse will often have a good roll and you will see how when it is on its back it wriggles around to scratch its back.

The same sequence of movement occurs when a horse rolls, except that as soon as it is on its side it uses its legs to create enough momentum and tries to roll over from one side to the other. Usually a horse should be able to turn from one side to the other. If it can't, then the ground may be too deep or sloping, the horse may just be too fat or it may be too old or weak.

Rolling also supposedly belongs to territorial behaviour. If I use the turn-out area of my liveried horses (which are not part of my resident herd) as a route for my pony herd to get to their own field I will often see the herd leader Eric have a roll on the "foreign" sand – although he has exactly the same kind of ground in his own turn-out only a few metres further on.

Rolling orgies
Some horses love rolling in big puddles or in water. This means being quick as a rider as lying down isn't always preceded by the usual pawing or splashing with the forelegs. By doing this the horse is checking out the ground underneath for being suitable to roll on.
My pony-cross will collapse onto her forelegs without any warning at all and plop down suddenly to lie down in the water – with rider and saddle intact – regardless of time of year. After doing this a few times we now avoid riding through any water at all …

This horse is clearly showing pain on its face: the eyes are narrowed and the nostrils and mouth are pinched. It is suffering from colic and is rolling from pain.

Pure pleasure: closed eyes and nose stretched out.

Horses will however also roll as a result of stomach pain and this is therefore an important sign of the start of an episode of colic. However, if you look carefully you will see a clear difference between the two types of rolling. When a horse rolls for pleasure and for coat care it will roll from one side to the other often several times and rub its neck and back on the ground before quickly standing up again and shaking itself. When it is rolling as a result of pain however an animal will often just lie on its side and appear to retreat into itself. Has the act of lying down itself relieved some of the pain or perhaps not? The rolling that then follows is not as extensive and without any pleasure but instead is more automatic. The horse then stands up and will often not shake itself as it would normally. Some just stay standing quietly, as if listening to their stomachs, will swish their tails and sometimes they will kick the back leg up towards the stomach. The horse's face will show a clear expression of pain. In the case of extreme pain they will lie down and roll again after taking only one or two steps; some will overflex their backs while lying flat on the side which is supposed to help relieve cramps in the stomach. Even veterinarians are themselves not sure whether a horse showing colic symptoms should be allowed to roll or not. Does the horse relieve the pain or does it worsen the situation? As a horse owner it is perhaps safer to allow the horse to lie down but try to prevent it from rolling and encourage it to walk around if it can.

Eliminating

Urinating and producing droppings (defacating) belong to this type of behaviour. These activities are of great significance in the life of the herd and serve much more than just the winary and digestive systems. Even if it isn't the most pleasant of subjects, defecating is one of the horse's behaviours that is most worthy of mention. Droppings are a source of information for horses, telling them when and who has been in any given area. Stallions especially will get a lot of information by smelling droppings and can tell from them which mare is in season from the secretions present from the mare's season in her droppings. Thus a stallion can tell – without risking being kicked – when it is worth trying to mate with the mare.

It is more likely for male animals to be interested in the droppings of their herd-mates but some mares do show some interest. Geldings and stallions will often exhibit specific behaviour both in the field and in their stables when it comes to producing droppings. As a way of marking their territory they will often defecate in the same place. In the stable it might be in the same corner which, for those who have to muck out, is a great advantage. Out in the field, dominant animals often like to defecate near or on top of their herd-mates' droppings in order to stamp their authority over their territory.

What the droppings themselves look like is also a source of a great deal of information for us about the health of our horses: are they firm, too soft, too light or too dark? Depending on what is being fed, all of this plays a role in monitoring your horse's health. Everyone knows that diarrhoea or very wet droppings are a bad sign. But droppings that are too hard or dark can indicate an irritation in the gastro-intestinal system which should be treated as quickly as possible.

It is also possible that a horse that is lacking in nutrition may eat droppings. If this happens then it is well past time to find out which nutrients are missing from its diet and also to check the quality of what is being fed.

It is not only the physical condition of a horse that can be interpreted from its droppings, but also its psychological state. Horses that are excited will tend to produce droppings more often. You can see this in a herd when it is galloping around as a result of excitement or stress and the horses produce droppings as they gallop. You also see this very often when horses are travelling, with many animals producing droppings as a result of excitement while they are being loaded onto their trailers or lorries.

When riding or working a horse in-hand a horse frequently producing droppings is a sign of excitement and as a rider you should consider whether you are asking too much of your horse or whether it may not feel comfortable for any other reason: is its tack causing pain, is it stressed because of any outside influences such as being separated from its friends or are you asking too much of it either physically or mentally?

Urinating doesn't play as much of a role for horses in marking their territory as droppings do, even if some male animals will sometimes urinate over a rival's droppings. When urinating male animals extend their hindquarters out behind them and move their forelegs slightly forward – almost resembling a saw horse and a bit like a horse with laminitis. On the one hand this position makes it easier for them to extend the penis and on the other it reduces the risk of the legs being sprayed with urine. Mares round their backs and widen their hind legs to urinate

with a raised tail. Whenever possible horses will seek a soft, absorbent surface on which to urinate as they don't like the urine splashing their legs.

Trailer therapy

If you are sure that your horse is starting a bout of impaction colic and its circulation is still in good order then a short trip on the trailer can work miracles. This saved my own mare a few years ago when my vet was stuck in a traffic jam. She suggested that I drove my mare, who was an experienced trailer traveller, around for a while. When I got back to the yard 15 minutes later there was a pile of poo behind her in the trailer and my mare was visibly relieved of pain. I was spared having to do a further such treatment when the vet finally arrived two hours later. But a warning – this doesn't replace a vet's visit and only serves as an option in the case of a very mild impaction colic, at least until the vet arrives.

This is the typical position when a mare urinates: the hind legs are spread and the back is rounded.

Male animals especially will smell droppings to find out who has been there before them.

Greeting rituals

Horses that are allowed to live in a stable herd, as opposed to those that are just turned out occasionally to graze together, are constantly and silently communicating with each other. The way they are positioning and holding their bodies, their ears and tail and tension around the mouth are all being used to tell the others what they are feeling. This is almost always connected with their physical space and who can stand where and who has to give way to the other.

The process of greeting unknown, but also known, horses will always follow a specific procedure. First of all the two will approach each other with pricked ears and curious expressions: visual signals dominate. If they like the look of each other, meaning that there are no threatening signs made, then they will sniff each other around the muzzle and finally around the neck and shoulder. Providing everything remains peaceful the nasal exploration will be extended to the flanks. Finally the udders or the genitals as well as the tail will be inspected via the sense of smell. Usually at the latest at this stage there may be a squeal of protest or some form of threat shown since horses that are meeting for the first time rarely take such a liking to one another that neither tries to exert dominance over the other. This desire to be the dominant one is usually what leads to some sort of display behaviour, which makes any further peaceful exploration of the other impossible. In extreme cases a real battle might result, with mares turning their quarters to each other and in the case of geldings or stallions starting with the forelegs lashing out and biting the other's neck. In both cases the person should stand well back so that he or she doesn't get caught in the middle. Even if there is a fence between them this can in itself be dangerous and cause serious injury, especially if the forelegs are used to lash out, or if one of the horses rears.

Introducing new horses into the herd

Introducing new horses into a herd can be very tricky and demands a lot of know-how as well as good instincts. To avoid injury you shouldn't just have one, but two fences between them at a distance of at least a metre. The horses won't be able to get too close and can get to know the others by sight and by smell at a distance. Turning new horses out for a few hours together and grazing and hacking out together are both good ways of them getting to know each other. Aggressive attacks against newcomers tend to occur usually in rest or play times.

Following the initial curious expression as they greet each other, depending on how much they like the look of the other, they will usually take on a more imposing impression with flared nostrils, tensed cheek muscles and even an opened mouth. At best the other will then react with a sign of submission such as laid-back ears. In the worst case the other will react with similar threatening signals.

Stallions show the greatest reactions to other stallions since they see in each other natural rivals. Friendships can develop between adult stallions but this is more the exception and restricted almost exclusively to horses that are not being used to breed, but rather being used just for riding.

The expressions here are typical of horses that are either meeting for the first time or after a long time apart. They obviously like each other: you can see this from the nose-to-nose contact, pricked ears, rounded necks and friendly expression in the eyes.

Although the grey has submissively laid its ears back the black pony has still reacted aggressively.

Display behaviour

If two stallions meet across a fence the display behaviour will range from loud whinnying, through to arched necks and heads held high through to passage and piaffe-like steps up and down the fence opposite each other. In some photo sessions, stallions may be put together for more impressive shots however the transition between showing off in play and actually fighting can be fairly fluid. It then becomes very dangerous for people to step in.

Even in the quietest of geldings you will sometimes see stallion-like behaviour when it meets a new herd member.

But even a mare will also react with an alteration in her silhouette by raising and rounding her neck, pulling in her nose towards her chest and appearing to become larger. Depending on how dominant the mare is, this silhouette will either disappear quite quickly and turn into more deferential behaviour or will turn into an attack – usually by turning round quickly and kicking out. Stallions on the other hand tend to lash out more often with the forelegs while rearing up against each other.

These alterations in the way a horse uses its body can sometimes be seen in a more diluted form around a yard when two horses of similar ranking that don't know each other are led past each other.

Variations in trot

Interestingly all of a horse's display behaviour takes place in trot whether it is the dancing steps of a stallion as it is led up to a mare; the elevated trot that even foals exhibit and that makes it look as if a horse has springs in its feet, with every step catapulting it up into the air; the passage trot that becomes piaffe when the horse is stopped from moving forwards. The stamp with its front foot that a horse makes when it is contained can also be seen as a vestige of the display behaviour in trot.

Someone is really showing off. The neck really couldn't be arched any higher and the tail is carried like a waving flag while the horse shows off its expressive trot.

Threatening expressions and behaviour

I am always surprised when I hear someone say that a horse has bitten someone for no apparent reason. Usually there is a sequence of threatening gestures that we often don't pick up: ears that are laid back are the clearest sign of a threat. Before this though a number of other signals are given such as the outer edge of the nostril being pulled back. If the lips are pressed together then you can clearly see how the mouth is pulled downwards before, in the next stage, a bite being threatened and then escalating to the mouth being opened and the incisors being shown.

The mouth may continue to show a threat of biting while the horse pricks its ears and turns its attention to something else, while internally still being programmed to attack.

When horses are able to move around freely when they start to look threatening there is also a clear change in the way that they are standing. Usually the horses will turn sideways on to each other with their necks arched to a greater or lesser degree. If an opponent shows no reaction then the head and the mouth will be used again to get a reaction before turning the quarters round for the next stage which is to either kick out or force the other to give in and back away. Sometimes this is preceded by a stamp of the foreleg if the opponent is perhaps naughty or stubborn but isn't supposed to be seriously hurt in the fight, such as, for example, in the case of foals or other cheeky herd members that don't submit to initial threats and don't want to give in. A further type of threatening behaviour is tossing or swinging the head back and forth which you will often see amongst horses. This is a clear sign of aggression which is not being expressed and instead is being suppressed.

Stallions and geldings will often drop their heads and necks low as a threatening gesture specific to them and always used towards mares. This position is used to better herd and drive the horses in front of them. A stallion will swing its head back and forth stretched out low over the ground with its ears laid back. This is an unmistakable gesture that allows no room for doubt. After just one day in the herd my Spanish horse exhibited this type of behaviour not just towards the mares but also towards the Shetland geldings and even towards me! It was only when I stood my ground did he come out of his "stallion trance" (as a gelding...) and show normal behaviour. This type of behaviour is rare in mares – unless they are protecting a newly born foal.

Besides the head, the hindquarters have a large number of interesting and powerful types of threatening gestures at their disposal. The nervous twitching of the tail which almost always has emotional significance, the back leg being lifted, the tip of the hoof being rested on the ground or the hoof lifting slightly to make a small kick into mid-air, through to a targeted and usually very accurate full-blown kick.

When playing, both hind legs will kick out but this is more an exuberant buck than a serious kick. It is also not meant to injure but is rather more intended for practice just as when two male animals play-fight together. In the wild, as male animals reach maturity, they will be forced to leave the herd. They will join with other young males to form so-called bachelor herds. These groups serve not only to protect against predators but also act as a form of training camp where they can practise their fighting techniques through play. The day will then come when one of them will face and defeat an aging herd leader to take over its herd of mares, or at least a proportion of them.

This shows the typical herding behaviour exhibited by male horses as this horse tries to drive its mares in front of it.

The normal threatening faces shown within a family: both of the other horses were resting when the little troublemaker came in from the left. It is shooed away clearly but not overly aggressively by the grey mare and it responds by submissively chewing.

Head-tossing as a typical sign of reluctance. You will often see this amongst horses when they are being herded or chased.

This Connemara shows initial threatening signs, albeit without wanting to fight. It is clearly saying "leave me alone".

Appeasing expressions and behaviour

Whether a situation escalates or not will substantially depend on the reaction of the lower-ranked horse. Even in the animal world there are certain strategies that will defuse the situation. The most typical of these is the open-mouthed chewing shown by foals. This can be caused in very young animals by the smallest of things or when encountering something new. The youngster will open and close its mouth with the teeth being clearly seen. Often you will also hear a clear smacking sound caused by the movement of tongue. It is usually reinforced by the head assuming a submissive position, the tail being clamped down and the horse looks as if it is trying to appear smaller. It will stretch its neck forward and straight ahead. The more uncertain a horse is, the more pronounced these signs will be. The more confident it becomes, the more they will fade until any signs of chewing shown will consist of the mouth being only slightly opened and closed. Even the most submissive of gestures will not stop some horses, especially those with underdeveloped social skills, from biting – unfortunately. It's worth noting though that horses that aren't part of a family group will react more violently than those that do belong to such a group.

You sometimes see this foal-like chewing behaviour in adult horses when they are greeting each other, as well as in stressful situations. When working with people licking is a remnant of this – more about this in the chapter on communication with people.

The position of the ears also plays an important role. The ears are held down and to the side to show submission, the degree to which this is done showing the degree of deference. If there are signs of resistance then they will be positioned down and back.

This foal is clearly showing the typical juvenile chewing gesture to placate the more dominant grey stallion.

This horse's entire body is expressing pain: the neck is held low, the eyes are half-closed, its ears appear to be trying to hear what is going on inside, it displays tense stomach muscles and a swishing tail.

Pain and illness

It is easy to tell from a horse's face whether it is feeling unwell. Beginning with its ears, moving on to closed or wide-open eyes through to the tension around the mouth, a horse's expression will show whether it wants to be left in peace. The ears will be turned back slightly, the eyes will be half shut so that the nostrils will be slightly pulled back. All of these are signals that it wants to be left alone. If on the other hand the mouth, ears and eyes are all relaxed and dropped down then the horse is likely just to be dozing.

Where the horse is looking will also give information about how the animal is feeling. If the horse is suffering pain it will almost appear to look inside itself. Its gaze will not be targeted at anything specific and not be fixed on its surroundings but instead appear to focus inwardly. The eye will appear tired and dull. You will see deep hollows above the eyes, often found in old, sick or unhappy horses.

The greater the physical pain or fear the less the ears will move. The animals appear to become virtually unaware of their surroundings.

> *Well observed*
> *My horses prove to me again and again that careful observation of your horses can really save you money. Often all it takes from me is one glance to see from either a facial expression, a swish of a tail or a horse lying down when it normally wouldn't to recognise the start of a colic episode. This means I can get the vet in early to administer a cramp-relieving injection rather than having to resort to a nasal tube or a visit to the clinic. Until the vet arrives you can help by keeping the horse quietly moving around and rugging it up.*

Wrinkles surrounding its eye, the nose pinched in: this shows an exhausted horse that shows its exertion by even sweating on its head.

When a horse is totally exhausted – whether from over-work, being chased as a new arrival in the herd or after a long and frightening trip on a trailer – you can see it clearly in its body and facial expression. A lowered head and sunken quarters are both a indications of its exhaustion. If the physical effort is recent then it will also be breathing heavily, which can be seen both in the movement of its flanks and stomach as well as its flared nostrils. Usually the eyes will be lacklustre and dull and half- or totally closed as well as appearing to be set deeper into the eye sockets. The hollows above the eyes will also be deeper and the ears will point backwards.

Vices

I use the word vice as a collective term for bad habits such as wind-sucking and crib-biting, weaving and box walking. They are also called stereotypical behaviours.

Wind-sucking means literally that a horse sucks air down its ocsophagus before releasing it out as a kind of burp. The air doesn't actually get to its stomach though. There are wind-suckers, more often called crib-biters, that bite into the stable door, fence or rails as well as those that don't need to make contact with anything and will wind-suck while standing still.

When a horse weaves it sways back and forth with its head and front legs. In extremely bad cases of weaving horses may also use their hind legs to balance out the movement. Bad weavers put excessive amounts of strain on their foreleg joints and this can lead to premature signs of wear and tear. Many horses that weave will also experience back pain and are trying to relieve their cramped back muscles by weaving. In this case the behavioural problem has physical rather than mental causes.

A horse that constantly walks in circles in its stable is said to be box walking. This doesn't mean just walking around once or twice to find the best place to lie down but rather doing it over a longer period of time. Constant movement like this in a confined space is bad for a horse's body and will cause muscle tensions and joint problems.

These types of stereotypical behaviours will occur in specific circumstances and are carried out almost obsessively. They are triggered by a horse being kept in unsuitable or poor conditions, by physical and mental stress, isolation or boredom. In the case of wind-sucking there is an increased chance of this being inherited as well as a link with poor feeding, stomach and heart problems. When wind-sucking the horse may be trying to regularise the rhythm of its heart again. If you tried to prevent this by putting a cribbing collar on it (this is a device that goes around the neck to prevent the tensing of the muscles needed to bite onto an object and suck in air) then the horse would have no chance of curing itself. There are horses that live out permanently or have plenty of turn-out and yet still weave and wind-suck. It can't be clearly proven either whether these behaviours are "catching" for other horses. You will however often see panicked reactions when a wind-sucker or weaver moves into a new yard. Crib-biting is one of the vices that must be declared when selling a horse.

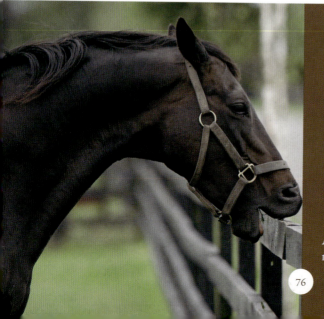

A typical crib-biter with the neck muscles tightly tensed.

Many vices are developed by horses when they are confined and their natural requirements for company and freedom of movement aren't met.

Fear

As an animal of flight and one that needs to live with others of the same species in a herd a horse is very quick to take fright. Fear and watchfulness are deeply rooted in these animals and are essential for their survival. How strong these instincts are though will depend partly on the breed and will vary greatly from horse to horse. Sometimes an animal might appear to be quieter than it really is and although it might be quaking inwardly it will show few obvious signs of fear. My Norwegian horses appear outwardly to stay calm in scary situations mainly because the breed tends to stand still rather than run away when they are frightened. But when you look into their eyes you can see the worry. When they do however decide to take flight they appear virtually to explode from all of the pent-up emotions and can be very difficult to control.

Situations that can cause a fearful reaction may be everyday activities that are unknown to a horse, from being tied up in a new place, saddled, training aids or different training situations through to a noisy tractor. But fear can also be caused by things or situations that have given a horse a bad experience previously. The best example of this is being loaded onto, and travelling in, a trailer. Unfortunately we can sometimes be so inept that the entire process is very traumatic for the horse. Instead of having a positive association from a young age, for most animals being transported is associated with stress, sickness, changing yards or competition and hard work. I would ask for your understanding that I am not going to go into great detail on the correct procedure since there are many good books and trainers that deal with the transporting of horses. I would however advise you to address this early on.

Other situations that cause fear tend to be of a more confining or constricting nature: being put in a crush at the vet's premises, tight spaces, bottlenecks, bridges – all situations in which the horse's ability to flee is either reduced or totally removed. Another challenging situation is when members of a herd are separated which may, depending on the individual animal's nature, be perceived as life-threatening.

In everyday life we experience many anxious moments usually simply when encountering new, unfamiliar things especially when they are associated with noise (vehicles, music, objects falling over, rustling tarpaulins and much more). I have only seen a horse show real fear towards another horse when it was being fiercely attacked in a very confined space and it couldn't get away.

If you have ever seen a horse that is really scared then you will be able easily to recognise it again. The more fear it is experiencing the more the eyes and nostrils will be widened. Some horses will even show the whites of their eyes. The entire jaw and mouth will be tensed.

The fear is not just shown in the horse's expression but throughout its entire body. The muscles will be tensed up, the tail will be held up and will not lie quietly, the head will be raised: every single fibre of its being is preparing to take flight. The horse will appear to grow bigger and will therefore also be even more alarming to its two-legged handler. They in turn will react through their body by becoming more uncertain and might even step back which again reinforces the danger to the horse. The more scared the animal is, the quieter and more confident you need to be in your own body language and be a reliable and trustworthy handler.

Sheer fear: eyes and nostrils wide open and mouth pressed firmly shut.

The quintessential picture of a frightened horse: restless ears, slightly widened nostrils that show its excitement, tensed mouth area and an uncertain gaze. It is asking itself whether it should run away or not.

The faces of play and fun

Even amongst horses you will find clowns and jesters. No wheelbarrow – especially when it's full – gate, broom or skip is safe. I have four of these horses in my own herd and typically it is one of these, Lasse, who has taken it upon himself to look after the foals and is doing a rather good job of teaching both of my filly foals, Pearl and Grazina, the great art of becoming herd jester – ha, ha, ha ...

I don't think there is any need for me to go into detail of what a horse that is up to mischief looks like – you can see it from the horse's alert expression with pricked ears, bright shiny eyes and quivering mouth. Amongst themselves playing will usually start by nibbling at another horse's mouth or cheek, often preceded by a session of mutual grooming.

Fun and games amongst geldings
Often my Shetland geldings will start to play together without the grooming session and just start to nibble the other's lips, moving up onto the shoulder before finally starting to nip the forelegs. At that stage when they will begin to chase each other some of the others are usually drawn in – although never involving more than three. And even then only for a short time as obviously three is one too many. A fun game of two chasing each other that may last as long as ten minutes usually comes to an abrupt end when a third one intervenes. When they are playing they circle each other excitedly and try and nip the other at the base of the tail – albeit with the often threatened kick coming to nothing. Foals often put in a two- or even four-legged buck. There is nothing better for me than to be able to watch my ponies really let off steam and play happily with each other, infecting others with their enjoyment and to be able to enjoy their speed and agility. Whilst the smaller, nimbler Shetlands seem to prefer fast chasing games, the larger horses tend more towards rearing games in which they drop down onto their front knee before standing up again, turning around each other and

then starting all over again by nipping the other on the mouth, leg and tail.
My Spanish horse, Valeroso, gets totally immersed in playing with his horseball all by himself. He picks it up with his mouth, throws it up, chases after it, kicks it – often by accident – away from himself and then follows after it. I watched him do this once for over an hour!

Mares are much more sedate. They really enjoy grooming each other and have their own special expressions when doing it. When they do another a friendly turn they stand alongside each other, head-to-tail or sometimes just up to the shoulder. They massage the whithers, neck, back or top of the tail by arching the nose forwards and moving it in circles sometimes with the addition of the teeth gently nibbling in the same area. Often they end up with clumps of hair in their mouths that then have to be spat out.

You can recreate the face that horses pull when being groomed by giving your horse a really good scratch in one of its favourite spots (knowing this is part of being a true friend to your horse). Beware though that it may try to return the favour which may involve using its teeth!

You can see similar signs if horses scratch themselves on posts, trees, stable walls or similar – their upper lip and nose extended forwards in ecstasy, ears tipped to one side and sometimes even having their eyes half-closed.

You will often see the nose extended out forwards or flared nostrils also when horses are playing together.

You can clearly see that someone is up to mischief: the eyes are open and full of curiosity, the ears are pricked.

This horse's curious and friendly gaze is focused in front and it approaches the photographer expectantly – there could be something interesting here or even a tidbit or two ...

Sexual behaviour

In season

A mare's season or oestrus occurs around ovulation. At this time mares will urinate more often than usual and the urine will smell particularly strong, due to the combination of urine and the secretions that occur as part of the oestrous cycle. It may smell strongly to us but for male horses it is more like an aphrodisiac. The actual period during which a mare can conceive and is receptive to mating is relatively brief and this is the reason why mares will show all the signs of being in season but won't let a stallion mount them.

You should bear in mind that some mares react particularly sensitively to the leg at this time. Often the fact that they are in season isn't recognised or taken into consideration and instead they are considered simply to be disobedient.

Love-sick
A mare can also be very insistent on her right to a love life when running in a herd. My mare, Mali, was desperate for a foal of her own and tried to force herself on any of the geldings that were of a similar size to her – especially the ones that were new to the herd. She made advances to the geldings, waving her bottom in their faces with lifted tail and vagina frantically blinking! When the geldings got fed up and marched off she would follow them around the field and would even forget to eat – and this from a genuine Fjord pony ...

The faces of mating

Very few horse owners are lucky enough see horses mating, unless of course they are breeders. A stallion will show obvious display behaviour towards a mare. The ears will be pricked, the nostrils flared and its entire body will be tensed. If a stallion and a mare come into direct physical contact then the stallion's behaviour will be determined by its temperament and personality. There are the tough machos, that mount the mare immediately and will bite the mate in the neck and mane, and then there are the more gentle ones that nibble the mare and are much gentler throughout. During the mating act itself both animals will appear to turn in on themselves, especially the mare. The mare will show that she is ready to mate by spreading her back legs and squirting out a thick yellow mucus combined with her urine. She also shows her readiness to mate by assuming a more passive expression on her face with ears turned to the side and back, mouth relaxed and a placid expression.

You can see this in a more diluted form in a mixed herd when the mare starts to come into season and there are geldings present that are interested in the opposite sex.

The attraction of something new
Up until now any newly arrived pony geldings have always shown serious interest in the few mares that I have. This naturally causes problems with the head of the herd who won't tolerate this. This results in the amusing situation when we clearly see how the newcomers, in co-operation with the mares, quietly and secretly try to outwit the supposedly dozing head of the herd – which of course doesn't work. Funnily enough the interest abruptly ceases once the ranking in the herd has been clarified and once they have secretly had their little fling with the mares – naturally behind the boss's back, usually when he has been working in the riding school. Following this initial flirt, in the years following few of the geldings will ever show real interest in the mares (except for my small 98 cm-high Jimmy) – even when they are very much in season and are virtually begging for attention.

The in-season mare signals her readiness by spreading her hind legs, lifting her tail and squirting a mixture of mucus and urine.

At the beginning of the covering the stallion acts in an extremely dominant manner to make the mare stand still. Some will even bite the mare in the neck. Although the mare has laid her ears back you can see that she is chewing as a young foal would.

It is lovely to see how the foal is trying to copy its mother.

Mother–child relationship

When it comes to a new mother, as a horse owner you should be aware that she will be much more ready to defend against and attack anything that in her eyes may be a threat to her foal – and that thing may be you.

Mother and child need anything from a few hours to two days until they are imprinted on each other. In this time it is important to give them as much peace and quiet as possible.

If the mare accepts her foal and lets it suckle without any difficulties then it will follow her everywhere, sticking close to the mare's side. If the imprinting isn't quite complete then the mare will need to follow her foal and direct it with a clear nudge of her nose towards her flanks. The surer a foal is on its legs and the more protective the rest of the herd is, then the more space foals will have to move about in. They will be able to make contact with other herd members without having to be protected by mum. Young mares particularly will sometimes have problems accepting their own foals. They don't instinctively look after them as a more experienced mother would and they have to slowly learn and grow into their new role as mother.

Behaviour – inherited or learnt?
I have often been able to observe how a mother passes on some of her character and way of interacting with others to her daughter. Pretty, a rather unobtrusive but friendly member of my herd, raised a similarly friendly filly foal that would take up contact with the other members carefully and in an open and friendly manner. Baschka, on the other hand, as a very self-assured member of the herd, brought her daughter up to meet any approaches from curious herd members with laid-back ears. Like mother, like daughter. This same observation has been noted by behavioural researchers. The lead mare in the herd is often also the daughter of a lead mare.

Where does my horse stand in its herd?

Whether a horse is dominant or shy is usually deeply rooted in its personality. These character traits permeate a horse's entire behaviour – whether in the herd, towards people or when carrying out new tasks either under saddle or in-hand.

Ranking in the herd

Your own horse's position in the herd will tell you a lot about its own self-image, whether it is confident or self-conscious and whether it approaches new things eagerly or with hesitation. For this reason in particular you should use the chance to observe how new horses integrate into an existing herd. This is a situation when a wide range of behaviours will be shown. Does my horse try and make contact with the newcomer, does it appear aggressive or threatening towards it or does it try to chase the newcomer away? If this is the case then your horse is likely to be more self-confident in nature. Does it on the other hand only trust itself to approach the new arrival in the company of the other horses? At the slightest sign of trouble does it retreat? If this is the case then you have an animal that is more uncertain about itself. There are though a multitude of possibilities: from the leader of the herd who makes it quite clear from the start who is in charge through to the lowest-ranking member who keeps well out of the new mix. The animals that tend to be more stressed when new members enter the herd are those in the middle. They tend to be unsure of themselves and worry about losing the position they have already attained to a new herd member who takes up a position higher up the herd hierarchy. These are the ones who experience real stress as then they experience a mixture of attack and flight.

There are also those horses that in relationship to us have to redefine their position. If you have made it clear to a horse that it comes second to you then it is usually quite happy in this position. It will though mean that any new person (trainer, owner or rider) has to prove him- or herself as a worthy leader. The insecure, sensitive type of horse will just be happy to have found a confident leader who has taken away the need for it to make any decisions itself.

In daily herd life though, even without the excitement of new members joining, there are also lots of signs which show where your horse comes in the herd hierarchy. In general the rule applies that everyone has to give way to the leader. Thus if an animal can move freely in the herd and all of the others make way then it is likely to be higher ranked. Is it always first to the feed and water or first through the gate? Does it have to give up its shady spot under the tree to another? Does it always have the best spot in the field shelter? Whoever gives way is always of lower ranking.

How secure and dominant a herd leader is within its herd is shown by the threats that it has to use to command respect. In the case of very dominant animals their very presence will suffice. This unconditional respect has often been hard and brutally won. Such dominant leaders tolerate no opposition whatsoever though. A more relaxed chief on the other hand has to reinforce its position constantly – usually by chasing especially the cheekier herd members away with laid-back ears to remind them of their inferiority.

If this isn't sufficient or they don't react quickly enough then a serious bite will follow.

As part of establishing its position in the herd the black is shoving the bay away with its hindquarters ...

Does your own horse give way to everyone else in the herd or does it chase others away? How relaxed or tense is its expression and how does it hold its ears? All of this tells us how our horse is feeling. How close does it stand to the others, does it appear to have a close friend, does it indulge in mutual grooming with one or many and does it have playmates? How close horses stand to each other can be an indication of how close they are emotionally as well.

In large herds that have constant movement in their members you will often see a form of resignation set in. The horses appear to be lacklustre in the way they establish their position – it will barely seem worth it as its "family" will change again soon anyway. Friendships will be rarer but enemies all the more dogged. Horses that have been sentenced to being "yardhoppers" by their owners will usually take little part in active herd life. You will be able to read their fate in their expression. They will appear resigned, the eyes will often appear dull and even quite young horses will have deep hollows above their eyes, even when they are physically healthy.

A difficult new start
I try as much as possible to avoid moving ponies in and out of my own herd for the good of the children and new riders who come to me who need a quiet, happy and secure group of ponies. The prerequisite for this is a stable herd that offers all of its members a sense of security.

Recently I took in two livery horses, a mare and a gelding, that were to move into a neighbouring yard. Both horses were therefore kept together when not out in the field with the herd and became very close. So close that when one of my mares made advances to the gelding the mare attacked it.

When the gelding suddenly had to leave my yard the mare was left by herself and had to be taken fully into my herd. Although she had been in close contact with the herd for nearly four months and

... followed by a kick with its hind legs.

had grazed with them freely in the field her integration proved to be harder than if she had come in totally new. When she had been protected by her gelding friend she had appeared to be very confident and self-assured. But after the protective gelding was no longer there she descended into a state of near depression that carried over to her ridden work with her owner. It was only my newest arrival, an Arab–warmblood cross, that got her out of it. Although at first it was seriously attacked by the mare, after observing the herd structure for a week it would drive the mare round gently but determinedly in its own kind of "join-up". The mare was very annoyed and would show this by lots of head-tossing and laid-back ears but allowed it. After two days the two formed their own dream team and since then the mare has been friendly, relaxed and willing to learn. The herd leader, Eric, who had never shown any interest in the mare at all kept himself well out of it.

There are also animals that are very strategic in their approach. In the first few days and weeks they appear to be relatively harmless, are friendly and open to everyone. Once they have had a chance to assess the situation and the structure of the herd the tables are suddenly turned and the friendly newcomer is transformed into someone that is after the lead position and is prepared to climb over the others to get to it. From one day to the next the horses that it had apparently made friends with will be chased and bitten into obedience so it can assume a higher position. Equine types like this will only often become active once they have formed a bond with another horse in the herd. And their tactics don't stop at fellow horses. They will watch carefully and use any weaknesses identified in the people around them to their benefit and to get their own way. These types are usually very intelligent and you need a lot of knowledge and empathy to get their cooperation.

A colourful and mixed herd that at first glance appears to be totally relaxed. The horse in front is rolling with great pleasure and the rest are dozing. Only the pony with the star appears to be getting a bit of stress from the chestnut that doesn't appear to like where the pony happens to be standing. The pony is already taking the first step sideways to get away.

The influence of rearing and upbringing

There are as many different types of equine personalities as there are types of people. And just as with us humans, personality is formed from a mix of inheritance, experience, education and social environment. Breeders can confirm that it isn't just conformation and appearance that are passed down from one generation to the next, but also character strengths and weaknesses. The genes are to a large extent responsible for this, but it is also the imprinting that occurs in the first few months of life, when the foal runs with its mother, that plays a role. As already suggested, foals appear to copy their mother's behaviour as well as that of any "aunts" that are helping with their upbringing.

Being raised in a mixed herd in which older animals contribute to the raising of the youngsters plays a significant role in ensuring that a horse is socialised and integrates easily with others of its species. Today it is common for youngsters and weanlings – usually at six months of age – to be kept with others of the same age in what is sometimes called a rearing herd. There may be plenty of good reasons for doing this from an organisational and practical point of view and the youngsters will have lots of playmates. For the social and psychological development of the individual animals though the effect is more negative since the experience and correctional role that the older generation plays is missing. There is no one to tell off the bullies or offer protection to the gentler or more timid members of the herd. Even worse and more devastating for the equine psyche though

A typical bachelor herd that is going off to explore the world.

is the oftseen phenomenon of a mare and foal alone in a field behind a house. The foal has no opportunity to learn about normal behaviour in a herd. Its ability to "talk" horse is often stunted since it only interacts with its mother and people. If animals raised in this way are suddenly introduced into a large herd because they are sold and have to live the life of a normal riding horse in a livery yard they often have great problems fitting in and making proper contact with the other horses. Simply put, they have language difficulties.

I can only advise anyone buying a new horse to enquire how the new member of your family has been raised. This might reveal potential problems that may occur later on during training, riding or competition. These problems might be physical in nature, such as if the horse hasn't had enough turn-out to be able to build up its strength and fitness, or has not been fed or cared for correctly in its early years. The problems may however also be psychological in nature such as if it hasn't had appropriate social contact with other horses. Horses that have grown up with little outside stimulation may react fearfully to everything that is new. On the other hand foals that have too active or unsettled a start can also exhibit very nervous behaviour. A healthy middle ground is the ideal – as in almost everything in life.

The effect of training on hierarchy

It may sound improbable but you can influence your horse's position in its herd by the way in which you work and train your horse. Horses that are constantly overworked or feel misunderstood and get frustrated will either channel this into increased aggression within their herd or will withdraw into themselves. If a rider ensures that their horse is proud in itself, makes the riding experience fun and the horse stays motivated and balanced both physically and mentally, this can have an effect on the horse's position within the herd. It will return to the herd more relaxed and happy. Horses prefer to surround themselves with good-tempered companions rather than grouchy ones. They are no different from us!

Sometimes our riding can cause our horses to feel real physical pain. By training the wrong muscle groups a horse can be put off balance or may never achieve real balance in the first place. This can then have an effect on its mental well-being also.

It shouldn't require as much physical effort as this to get your horse to yield and show respect. Cigarettes don't belong anywhere near a horse!

Different horse types

Genuine horse people quickly see what type of character they have to deal with. Lots of small details give them clues. Does the horse immediately give way to its handler or does it barge on through? How does it look at people – challenging, curious, confident or hesitant with flicking ears and with great attention? Does it come up to you in the field or does it wait, hesitate or even walk away? These initial impressions give you a glimpse into its soul. In-hand work is even better for observing and finding out more about a horse's character.

It all starts with the approach. Does the horse stand still, looking at the person, scanning them for treats, pushing them to the side to try and take their place or even walk over the top of them? If you are ever in this position then you are either dealing with an extremely confident, high-ranking horse – or one that is just badly mannered and has never learnt to enter into a dialogue with people.

Pretend strength

Often bad manners aren't a sign of cheekiness but rather of insecurity. If a horse has never learned to trust a human then it has to look after itself – someone has to! Together with bad manners and supposed cheekiness many such animals will often be quite fearful when faced with something new, such as new objects used for training or new movements. The confidence that masks their uncertainty will disappear in an instant.

If a horse flinches back when you try to touch it, or twitches its ears and tail nervously then you are dealing with a very insecure horse. Whether this insecurity results in the horse retreating to the extent that it pulls back and tries to run away or alternatively decides to attack will depend on the degree of pressure exerted by the handler as well as their ability to deal with a situation such as this. What the horse does in terms of stepping over the line can be predicted by observing all of the expressions and actions that have already been detailed in this book. The movement of the ears, the muscles around the mouth and the eyes are all indicators of a horse's mood. It is only when you don't react to any of these signs in some way that the rest of the horse's "body" language comes into play to state its point move clearly – in other words by biting, kicking, fleeing or breaking away.

It would be going too far to detail minutely every single thing that helps to interpret what a horse is trying to say. It is all too dependent on other factors. I can only recommend that you continue to observe your own and other horses carefully. Take time to carefully watch trainers when they are working with horses – especially when the training is quiet and harmonious rather than done with a lot of shouting, equipment and violence.

Communication with people

Up to now we have been learning the vocabulary of our horse's body language and the grammar of it in context with other horses. Now we can try and apply what we have learned to ourselves and our work with our horses. Besides a horse's own way of expressing itself a horse will also "read" and interpret our human body language. Many people are either not aware of the effect their own body language has on their horse or they interpret it totally incorrectly and so will be inadvertently giving out the wrong messages. In these cases a good trainer and a video camera can be really useful.

This book is not supposed to teach techniques for in-hand work or riding but rather aims at making you more sensitive to what your horse is bringing to the relationship. This should allow you to identify mistakes early and above all help you look to yourself, rather than your horse, when things don't go to plan. After all, who is it that claims, in evolutionary terms, to be the cleverer and the intellectual? Shouldn't we then be prepared to learn the language of our supposedly dumb equine partners?

Mood barometer

It would be the ideal if we were always feeling happy and positive when we went to ride or work our horses. This just isn't always the case. Due to our busy lives our horses sometimes become a chore that "have" to be ridden or mucked out. In the best case having to ride or look after our horses after a stressful day at work will lift our bad mood and make us feel rather better.

The chances for success in your work with your horse are much better if you start out in a good frame of mind. Anyone who has horses should always consider several things, as discussed in the following sections, before they start working with them.

How am I feeling?

Am I stressed, tense and rushing back from work? Have I just been annoyed by something at work? Am I lacking energy, totally uptight, feeling unwell and close to tears? None of these is a good basis from which to start doing anything with a horse. Grooming or taking your horse for a relaxed walk will probably be the best option. Even just lungeing or loose schooling might not have the best of outcomes if you tried it when feeling less than 100 per cent as these particular activities actually require a lot of concentration and an ongoing dialogue on both sides.

Am I feeling well and full of energy, am I in a good mood and feel ready for physical activity and do I feel "centred"? These are the best prerequisites when wanting to try out something new or complicated with your horse.

Every fibre of the human body is constantly expressing your current mood: hanging or straight shoulders, shuffling or swinging steps when you walk, standing up straight, smiling, erratic movements, lethargic, standing with two feet firmly planted on the ground, crossing your legs, nervously jiggling about – all of these are signs of how you are feeling. Even if we have almost forgotten, at least consciously, how

The person's body language here is showing a degree of caution.
The two mirror each other brilliantly.

to read these signals and to use them in making decisions in our daily lives many of us do subconsciously register them. Horses and other animals though rely on them to be able to understand and deal with us. The hard truth is that they are the ones that really have all the work to do when it comes to communicating and have to make allowances for us, rather than us for them – whether it be by refusing to work or by showing cooperation.

Sensitive antennae

Try and be aware of your own mood and that your body is telling your horse exactly how you are feeling. Your horse will always be a reflection of you – the good and the bad.

How is my horse feeling?

Horses have exactly the same mood swings and good and bad moments as we do. If your horse is out in the field with others you should take a moment to watch it and see what sort of mood it might be in. Is it chilling out and standing or even lying down; has the heat sapped all of its energy; is it saturated from constant rain or has it just found the tastiest patch of grass? These aren't the ideal prerequisites for a motivated and enthusiastic horse if you were then to get it in to ride. Often you can't do anything about it and have to interrupt your horse's life so that it fits into your schedule. However you have to be prepared that you will have to motivate it rather more than usual to ensure that both of you get something out of the session.

If you are prepared to look and feel your reward will be a devoted and attentive horse.

On the other hand, your horse may be standing, bored, in the field or is perhaps waiting for you at the fence. It is even better if your horse comes across to you as this is a sign that either life in the herd is really boring or that the horse really enjoys the work you are doing.

Animal welfare

Horses that are stuck in a stable for 24 hours are day are almost always happy to come out and do something – anything in fact! This is a fact that is sometimes intentionally used in some competition yards in order to always have motivated horses. To be honest I find this questionable and positively cruel in terms of animal welfare. This isn't how horses should be kept and is actually in breach of the animal welfare legislation.

A good start

Many people who have problems getting their horses in from the field cause the problem themselves by how they are doing it. They march straight up to the horse front on and this is exactly how predators approach their prey in the wild. Often you are carrying a halter in full view which is something that scares off a "soured" horse even more. If a horse doesn't enjoy its work – for whatever reasons – it will connect a number of objects with this work, including the openly presented halter. Try this instead – go out to your horse without anything at all. Stand next to it, stroke it and perhaps even give it a treat and then go away. If a horse can interact with a person for no other reason than just a pleasant contact with no connection to work then catching it will become easier. When

If your horse approaches you like this, curiously and positively, then the signs are good for a successful and enjoyable ride.

you do then really need to get it in to ride, it will trust you more if you put the halter over your shoulder and rather than marching straight up to it, go past it and approach it in an arc. Stroll rather than walk too briskly and don't look at it directly but rather appear to be interested in something else entirely. Alternatively go to another horse and stroke it. This almost always gets your horse's attention.

I like to stand two or three metres or even further away from the horse with my shoulders turned to the side and don't look directly at it, waiting to see if it comes to me. This is the first indication of how much it wants to do something with me. In almost all cases it will prick its ears, look curious and come up to me. Only then will I move towards it, put the lead rope over its neck and put the halter on over its head. I sometimes bite into a carrot to make the really

stubborn ignoramuses curious, to make myself, in the true sense of the word, palatable! Be careful though as this can cause problems with the other horses in the field.

For me, my work with a horse starts the very moment when I go to get it in from the field or out of its stable. Not just to see what sort of mood it is in but also through my own behaviour to get things on track for the work to follow.

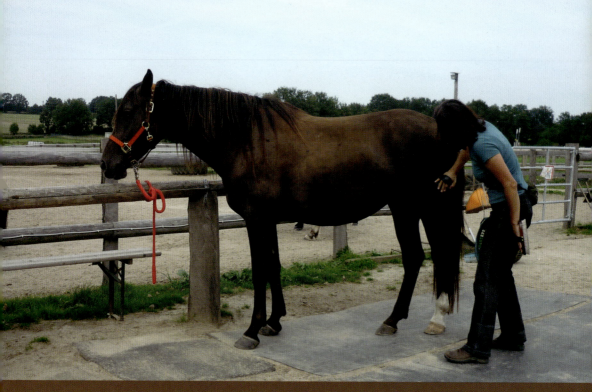

The mare is constantly "watching" her owner, with her ears. Her mouth is slightly showing a pleasurable expression typical for grooming and her eye is open and calm. (Photo: Daniela Bolze)

Grooming

Even when being groomed, horses send out lots of signals. Beginning at the ears, a mouth closed with pleasure, tensed muscles through the entire body, resting a hind leg or nervously swishing the tail and not standing still, all of these signs are telling you something. If you watch your horse carefully you will quickly find out which brush it prefers, what pressure it likes and which part of the body a horse doesn't like being brushed on.

My Fjords all enjoy being brushed and massaged really firmly with a hard bristled brush. If I tried to do this to my satin-skinned Spaniard, Valeroso, or even just approached him with this instrument of torture he would explode. For him and his silky coat only natural hair brushes and sheepskin grooming pads are just about good enough.

Every horse has its own individual areas that it particularly likes being brushed and stroked. Every horse owner should take the time to find where they are. Your horse will tell you when you have found one by showing a relaxed posture, slightly closed eyes, and ears turned slightly to the side. Often it will rest a hind leg as well. Some horses will turn their quarters to you because they particularly like being scratched at the top of their tail and over their quarters. If you aren't used to or ready for this it can look as though they are threatening to kick – they aren't, they just want you to scratch them. Our foals tend to do this a lot as we have spoilt them by doing this for them since they were born.

The attempt to get this Fjord pony to lift its front foot is unsuccessful since its attention is somewhere else. In addition it is resting the near hind so would find it difficult to lift the near fore anyway.

(Photos: Daniela Bolze)

Now that the girl has got her pony's attention she can pick out its hoof without problems.

When grooming you should not only always keep an eye on your horse, but it should always be keeping an eye on you. Its ears or at least one eye should always be turned towards the person handling or grooming it so that it knows where they are and doesn't accidently stand on their foot or jostle them. If I notice that the horse's attention is somewhere else I will speak to it or ask it to move its quarters round. This mutual attention will also simply help to prevent accidents happening.

Moving on to where you are tying the horse up to groom or tack it up, there should be no brooms, rugs, rakes or other things that can fall over or off anything and scare the horses. What the horse is tied up to needs to be strong and able to sustain a horse pulling back. If this is not the case then you shouldn't tie your horse up there. Generally speaking it is never a good idea to leave your horse tied up alone so ensure that you have everything for grooming or tacking up ready before you start.

Picking out feet is always a good indicator of whether you have a well-disciplined horse. It is always a good idea to pick feet out in the same order every time so that the horse has a chance to cooperate and join in. Usually you will find that it will lift its foot before you ask for it. If you have problems then it is either a sign that it is in pain or that it has no respect for its handler. Very timid or hesitant people will often

have problems convincing a horse to lift its feet up for them. On the one hand their body language is often too uncertain and unclear; on the other hand as an animal of flight it requires a lot of trust for a horse to stand on three legs. The person asking it to do this therefore has to be trustworthy.

If you own a young horse and are not confident yourself, find someone who is and ask them to teach your horse to lift their feet for picking out – this sets the pattern for the rest of its life and ensures that it is a pleasant rather than stressful activity.

Situations where horses are tied up close to one another, thus giving them the opportunity to squabble, are where accidents can happen as it is all too easy for people accidentally to get caught between them at the wrong moment. It is therefore so important to keep an eye on your horse at all times even when doing something as harmless as grooming. If you don't intervene in time with a quiet word or by asking your horse to move across it is all too easy for it to be "overlooked" and either jostled by another more aggressive horse or be on the receiving end of a kick that wasn't intended for it.

When grooming the tummy you will also be able to see whether there may be problems when saddling up. If the horse starts to lift its leg, twitch its tail or even lay its ears back when it feels the brush then you can assume that it is not going to like being girthed up.

Shetland pony, Fiete, is sensitive about having his girth done up and shows this by putting his ears back and swishing his tail. (Photos: Daniela Bolze)

In addition to the previous threats, the pony now lifts his head and tries to snap at his rider. Tessa is used to this and is thus very careful.

Saddles and bridles

If a horse has a problem with its saddle it will start to show this by stepping to the side when you approach with this item. If it does this you should give pause for thought and at least check that the saddle does fit correctly and go over the horse's back carefully for any signs of pain or sensitivity. Many people overlook these first signs that there may be a problem. Apart from being a sign that there may be a problem with the saddle or that it doesn't like being girthed up, it can also be a sign that the horse has a problem with its work.

In the best case a horse will just kindly be making room for its rider to be able to put the saddle on. If this is the case then the horse's ears and mouth will stay relaxed and the tail won't swish.

It is therefore worth carefully watching how the horse physically reacts to you or others, no matter what you are doing. So-called horse whisperers and gurus do nothing else but this. They break down any interaction with a horse into small units and then observe and register the smallest of reactions.

A horse that bucks because it is in pain will give indications of this when being saddled up, and not just wait until it is ridden. You just shouldn't miss seeing these signs.

The majority of horses are unbelievably fair to us. They make their intentions very clear. It is only when we don't react to any of these clear signs that they resort to means that we cannot ignore. Who should we blame – those that don't hear or those that are trying to express their unhappiness in so many ways?

The same applies to putting a bridle on. If you can do it so that the horse opens its mouth for the bit rather than just pressing the cold metal against its teeth then there shouldn't be any problems, especially if it is immediately rewarded with a treat. If however the horse always lifts its head up high or tries to avoid the whole process then you should check the bit for sharp edges and that the bridle fits correctly. It is also just as important to have a horse's teeth checked regularly and that the canine teeth aren't causing problems.

In winter it can also be a good idea to warm up an ice-cold bit a little before you stick it in your horse's mouth. You can do this either by just holding it in your hands or sticking it under your jacket for a short while. Warm water can also come in handy! But do be careful that you don't heat it up too much.

Saddle problems
A horse owner once asked me for help. Her mare would bare her teeth when she entered the stable with the saddle. I asked her to put the saddle down and she could then walk up to her mare with no problems whatsoever. The mare however showed a lot of pain at the slightest touch to her back by swishing her tail, flinching away from the touch with her back and laying back her ears. When questioned, the owner confirmed that the problem had got gradually worse – from not standing still, tail-swishing, biting, kicking and pulling back when tied up. It had got so bad that you had to dodge her in the stable because she was getting worse. Obviously nobody was able to interpret the increasingly desperate signs that the poor mare was giving to express her pain. And we won't even discuss what she was like to ride ...

Leading and working in-hand

I am continuously amazed at how many owners think leading a horse means pulling it along from point A to B. This rather disharmonious-looking scene is often unfortunately continued on into riding and is a good example of a lack of communication.

For horses, the question of "who is moving whom" is one of the central themes in their lives. We should therefore concentrate on this and learn and use some of their own easy techniques because they contribute so much to a clear, safe and harmonious relationship.

Fortunately over the last few years there are many good trainers who have specialised on in-hand work utilising correct body language and communication. Rather than go into detail on the correct technique for leading I would like to fine-tune what you are hopefully already doing. For horses being led is all a matter of trust and dominance. It is something that they do constantly with others in a herd without either lead rope or halter. We use these things for reasons of safety in case our horse breaks off our conversation and tries to run away. Leading occurs as a result of the correct positioning of your body combined with the correct balance of driving and braking.

Rather than being aggressive or wary most horses that have not been taught to lead correctly tend more to just do their own thing. They will barge at one moment, let themselves be pulled along the next or just march on when you actually want to stand still. All of these are clear signs that the hierarchy hasn't been set or rather that the horse sees itself as the one in charge. This makes it all the more important for clear boundaries to be set by using body language that is clear and has unmistakeable meaning. This can be anything from a sharp tug on the halter, carrying a whip in front of the horse – whether it be just to wave it in front of it, prod it in its chest or even, in the case of particularly "deaf" ponies, banging the handle of the whip against their noses – to waving the lead rope in order to drive particularly bad cases forwards. Once it is clear what you want, the horse should relax and follow.

Starting out right
With foals, you can set them on the right path for the future and start training them to lead early, albeit very carefully. In the case of my foal, Pearl, I made some serious mistakes. We started out well as a threesome with the main focus on her quarters, with a rope around her rear or someone pushed her from behind if needed. When I wanted to have more control over her head though and more influence with the lead rope I allowed myself to become part of a tug of war which resulted in Pearl falling over. We were both exceedingly surprised and since then she has become a very hesitant horse to lead as she views the whole thing very suspiciously. Grazina, on the other hand, is very different. I learnt from my mistakes and started by only leading her in confined spaces so that she never developed any inclination to try to get away as there was simply no room for this to happen. Her mother, Baschka, was always alongside her. There was never any sign whatsoever of resistance and she always followed obediently. This trust associated with people is so ingrained that she has never questioned it. If we meet something scary or unfamiliar, such as cars or a tarpaulin, after a slight hesitation she will always trustingly follow me. I don't however ever try to pull her, but rather wait and stay calm.

It is important to be very picky and precise when it comes to where you stand and where your horse is positioned. You can ask your horse either to stay behind the person leading or walk with its shoulder or its head beside you or even in front of you. Which position is selected will depend on where you are – loading, in traffic, in a bottleneck and so on. What is important is that the position chosen is maintained until the person leading decides to change it.

Essential pickiness

It may only be one step, or even only half a step that dominant horses will try to take but this will determine whether they are being led or are the leaders. After halting going one step more, regardless of whether it is forwards, backwards or to the side, trying to overtake the person leading or walking off before asked – all of these are tests. You need to know this if you really want to be in charge. Even if one step really isn't that important for me, it is for the horse and has to be prevented. The best way of doing this is by being so dominant in my attitude that the horse doesn't dare try taking this one step. You need to use very clear body language. If it takes a step then I get it to step back to where I stopped it or positioned it and thus it gives me my step back.

When working in-hand you have a wonderful opportunity to see your horse's reactions exactly since you can see all rather than just part of it as you can in the saddle. How does it react to new things, how quickly does it react and how does it express fear, curiosity or a lack of enthusiasm?

You can see from a horse's expression whether it is afraid, insecure or doesn't want to work. You need to react accordingly. If a horse is really lacking in enthusiasm then I will be much more forceful than if it is fearful. If two horses refuse to do something they may show very different reactions. A horse with its eyes wide open and mouth tense is showing fear and insecurity. Whenever I work with a horse I have to be certain that it is actually listening to me.

This young Fjord pony doesn't have its attention on the girl and instead is focused on something in front and has taken over the leading.

This is a good example of safe leading over unknown territory. The horse is dealing with the tarpaulin with an attitude of curiosity rather than fear: she stays in the correct position in relation to the person leading her and is showing confident body language.

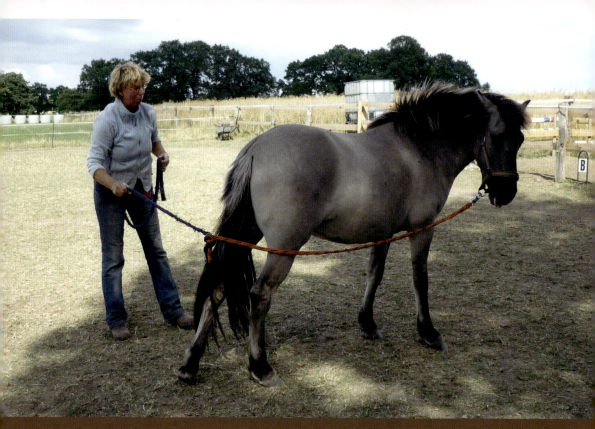

In this rather improvised rope exercise Baschka is being asked to give her head and turn her quarters. At first she hesitates and doesn't understand what she is being asked to do. As I maintain a slight pressure on the rope she yields and begins to lick. Praise immediately follows in the form of the rope being dropped as well as verbal praise. (Photo: Daniela Bolze)

What do licking and chewing mean?

When working in-hand the way the ears move, the mouth and the eyes all play an important role. Especially in the case of the mouth the horse may lick or chew to show that it is mentally yielding or relaxing. Perhaps it is a left-over from the submissive foal chewing action which we have already discussed. In the case of round-pen work (sometimes called into question because of the immense pressure it may involve) licking of the lips is always a trigger to ask the horse to come into the handler. It is seen as a sign that at that moment the horse has "submitted" itself to your dominance. To me it is always a sign that a horse has recognised some

form of regimentation or rule and accepted it. It represents a kind of peace sign or sign of submission. If a horse licks its lips then I immediately remove any pressure and praise it. Usually you see it when you ask a horse to back up as a way of disciplining it. Or when you have been building up pressure and the horse suddenly gives in. If a horse has snapped at a person or tried to run them over and is punished for doing this then licking is a kind of surrender. Following this you can then go back to being neutral and work on positively. To me, maintaining the pressure after a horse has yielded and licked its lips is just rude and leads to misunderstandings. I would like to have a sensitive and cooperative horse – and this means being fair. If a horse yields to me – either physically or mentally – then I have to accept this offer of communication if I want to ensure that we have a meaningful conversation. The most effective and readiest of praise is a release of pressure. If, despite this, I carry on then for the horse it is pointless to listen or yield

as the pressure continues anyway. It will either become uncooperative and stubborn or unsure. In the worst case it will simply resist all contact with people.

Lungeing

Lungeing with either one or two lunge lines is an important stage in the training of a riding horse. I will assume that you know how important body language and the position of the person conducting the lungeing is as I don't have room here to go into detailed instruction. There are many good books that cover this specific topic. Here I am looking at how the horse expresses itself during this type of work.

If lungeing is taking place in either a round pen or lungeing pen, and since the lunge line itself confines the space used, it is possible to exert immense pressure on a horse if you don't do it correctly.

Join-Up®

Classic Join-Up® usually takes place in a confined space, often a lungeing or round pen. The horse is sent away from the handler who uses more or less pressure created from a combination of the handler's body position, tension and a long rope thrown towards the horse to drive it on. For insecure horses this can be very frightening. Higher-ranking horses that feel threatened may even be provoked enough to try and attack the handler.

As a herd animal a horse will always seek the company of others – in an emergency even that of unknown people. In order that they are the boss of their own herd, in Join-Up® the handler will drive the horse away just as a herd leader would to a newcomer. Since it will instinctively want to be close to someone it will try and approach them, which can then be allowed. It sounds easy but for a horse it is fundamental and when done incorrectly can do a lot of damage.

You should always choose a fenced, safe area for lungeing. If you use somewhere open many horses will try to pull and get away. This can be painful for the mouth or bridge of the nose, depending on where you have the lunge line fastened, and can also be quite painful for the lunger's hand if he or she is not wearing gloves. I have heard of some people who have lost fingers because the lunge line became wound around their fingers and the horse ran off.

You should therefore be very careful when lungeing and ensure that young horses are taught to lunge by someone who knows what they are doing.

When lungeing you can observe the horse while it works. I am able to see when it suffers either physical or mental tension or equally when it relaxes. I can see how well it is swinging through its back, how far the hind legs are stepping through and whether the tail is swishing nervously back and forth or whether it is relaxed and swinging.

A prerequisite for any dialogue with a horse is again having its attention. When lungeing or loose schooling the inside ear should always be fixed on the handler. If this isn't the case then you need to get it by using your voice or lunge whip. If the horse's ears are constantly focused on things other than the handler, then you need to check whether the area being used is quiet enough for undisturbed work, whether the horse is stressed in some other way (is sick, has just changed yards or has problems in the herd, or too much is being asked of it) or whether the wrong signals are being given by the handler.

This horse is moving loosely and in a relaxed way with a rounded back and is working in a Chambon. Its inside ear is fixed on the person with the lunge line. The two are mirroring each other in terms of their concentration and confidence.

If the handler is asking the horse to do things that either scare it or make it feel insecure then it will turn its head and try to look at the handler with both eyes. It may also toss its head. If the handler continues to exert pressure and drive the horse forward it may turn its quarters in and try to kick out at them and then take off bucking. This isn't the best of climates in which to work. Abruptly changing direction is also a sign that the horse is either finding it all too much or has no enthusiasm, but it is also a sign of an animal trying to show dominance over people.

In these cases I would recommend going back a step: either by going down a pace (e.g. from canter to trot) or working in the same pace but using less pressure with either your body or whip and ensuring that that the horse starts to relax again. Lungeing in walk is really only possible when the horse is totally relaxed.

Quick starters
My Spanish horse loves to move and so at the start of any session I let him chose the pace. This means that he usually sets off happily in trot. As he lives out he isn't exactly starting cold so I don't worry about his muscles being strained. When I first got him I used to try and insist that he started at the walk and the result was a horse that was totally tensed up. By being able to select his own tempo, within three or four circles he has settled down and then responds to my commands. If he needs to walk first for health reasons then I lead instead.

If the horse tends to run away out of control then you may need to move back to leading work when you can be closer to the horse. You can transmit more calm to the horse and have it carry out small commands successfully before gradually moving further away until you are once again working on a longer lunge. It is always

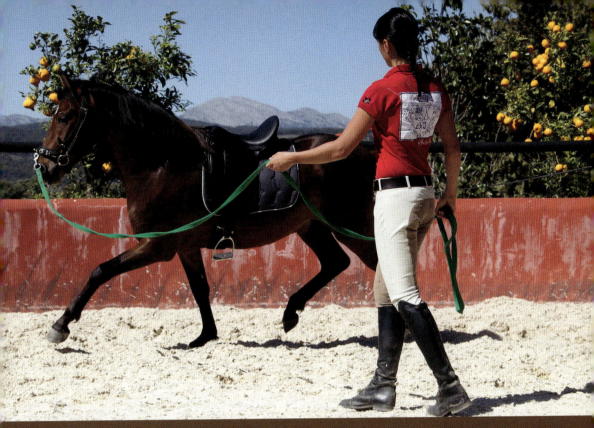

Here a young horse is being lunged for the first time. You can see clearly from its facial expression, body and the prominent muscle underneath its neck how tense it is.

A short time later it explodes, striking out in front, swishing its tail and its face is showing clear signs of stress.

wise to keep an eye on any tension in the mouth, under-neck and tail areas. The faster you can recognise this tension occurring then the quicker you can react.

To set the tempo on the lunge requires a great degree of knowledge and ability from both horse and handler. Although you can control the space in which the horse is moving thanks to the lunge line, this is harder to use to stop or slow the horse if it really doesn't want to listen. The person lungeing therefore only has their body and its position available to stop or slow the horse down or they can make the circle smaller by shortening the lunge line and gradually bring it into the centre. Both of these can interfere with the horse's balance and regularity of movement.

You can get good results by watching which pace the horse prefers to go in when you start lungeing. Before it even moves into trot or canter give the appropriate verbal command and then praise. Do the same when moving down in pace. You are therefore making what the horse is thinking of doing your own idea. To do this though you have to watch very carefully and pick the right moment. Is it lifting its head and shoulder to get more impulsion to go faster or is it dropping them to go slower? In this way you are staying in charge because the horse is doing what you have asked and can be praised for doing it. Praise creates a pleasant and motivating work environment. The more a horse learns the commands, the more relaxed you will be and able to ask for any of the paces at any stage without stress or tension.

To be able to lunge correctly and effectively, above all you need to understand and observe exactly how a horse moves, i.e. its movement mechanism. You need to know whether it is relaxed or tense and how actively or aggressively it reacts. Whether a horse finds specific work stressful or enjoyable can be seen not only by the tense or relaxed muscles in its neck but also by its facial expression. Does it have its ears laid back, is it tense around the mouth and are its eyes wide open or narrowed to a slit? Not good. If the horse has screwed up its nostrils and

turned its ears back then it is likely just to be fed up. You often see this in horses that are in convalescence after becoming lame and their only exercise is to be lunged for weeks on end. The reluctance appears on their face even before they get to the lungeing pen. Quite rightly too, as going round in circles is exceedingly boring.

You should also look very carefully at a horse's face when you are using side reins. If they are too short or you use them too early on in training and before the horse has really established its balance then they can cause real panic. Always start with them longer and then gradually shorten them rather than putting them on too tight initially. When a horse is scared it opens it eyes wide and the neck will stiffen, especially the muscle underneath the neck, and the back will be pressed down ready for flight.

An arch of suspense

When a horse is either physically or mentally stressed, first of all the muscles in the jaw tense, followed by those in the poll and their counterparts in the muscles underneath the neck. Every muscle that is tense, and thus working, is being trained – even those in the lower part of the neck that we don't want to develop. Lungeing and riding are supposed to strengthen the back and not the muscles underneath the neck. You must therefore ensure that these can relax in order to work the stomach muscles that support the back. Since the muscles from the tail to the top of the neck are all connected this means that, when the muscles underneath the neck contract, the back will hollow. If you can get the neck to stretch forwards and down, then the back muscles will also be stretched.

As well as getting away from work by taking flight and galloping off, horses can also just stand still, turn to the handler and start at them. In the first case you need to re-establish trust and go back a step before you make the work area too large and go too fast. When a horse turns in it might be due to a misunderstanding. The handler may have expressed themselfes with their body and whip so unclearly that the horse just doesn't understand what they want. Higher-ranked horses or very self-confident ponies like turning in. In the best case they are asking for clearer instructions, usually shown by their ears being pricked forwards. In less ideal cases they will try to get away or may even try to attack. In this case the ears will be pinned back, the area around the mouth will be tense and the nostrils will be wrinkled up. Horses that are as dominant as this belong in the hands of experts! For this reason I won't even try to make suggestions on how to solve this problem as it could lead to serious injury.

How a ridden horse expresses itself

When ridden a horse will still be sending out information about how it feels, whether it is having fun or feeling pain and whether it is being asked to do too much or too little. You need to be ready to listen and to feel. There can be differences from day to day. Sometimes the steps are tenser, sometimes more relaxed. Sometimes the paces are hurried, sometimes lazier, such as on a hot summer's day. Besides this though there are other clear signs that must not be overlooked.

Tempo

If a horse either rushes or is not at all forward-going then this might be a sign that there is something wrong. When a horse rushes there is usually a problem with a horse's balance. In order literally to try to catch up with itself it uses speed as an escape, not only in the case of imbalance in the physical sense but also in the mental sense. If a horse is finding a movement too difficult then it may also react by going faster. The extreme of this is a horse bolting, when any control of the horse's speed is lost and it grabs the bit and runs. This usually happens when out hacking as there is plenty of space in which to run and there are plenty of outside stimuli that can scare a horse. It can also occur in an arena. The limited space can help to get the horse under control but it can also cause other problems, such as the horse falling over with its rider when trying to turn too quickly. In addition a horse taking off, which in itself isn't overly dangerous, can turn into much more dangerous bucking and rearing.

Other horses react to physical and mental problems by going more slowly and withdrawing into themselves. Horses like this appear not to listen and are preoccupied within themselves, reacting even when tied up to few outside stimuli. If it reaches a stage when the horse won't move at all then this has been preceded by a long process of suffering during which no one has listened to it. The first signs of any reluctance to go forwards are usually met with stronger aids to which the horse then becomes immune. This is a vicious circle which it is difficult to escape from and to do so needs a great deal of expertise.

Here – just as with running off – it is essential to check the horse's health and equipment. Are there problems with its back, muscles, joints or teeth? Does the saddle fit and is the bit appropriate, does the bridle fit well behind its ears and does the saddle cloth rub or press where it shouldn't? There are unfortunately so many things that can cause problems that sometimes the search for the cause takes a long time and can be expensive but for the good of the horse it is worth it.

Looking for mistakes

If a horse moves normally in its daily life and the only time that it starts to go lame is when being ridden then something must be wrong. Making it go more forward, which is often the response, doesn't solve the problem and can make it a lot worse. In these cases you need an expert that can more thoroughly look for the reasons, whatever they may be – mental or physical overload, health or dominance problems or unsuitable equipment.

If the horse tries to get away from the aids by taking off then a health, equipment and riding check is necessary.

Here it looks very different: in canter the horse is on the aids on a light contact and its attention is focused on its rider who quite rightly looks as if she is having fun.

Tail-swishing and tossing of the head usually precede a buck with two or four legs leaving the ground.

Bucking

Bucking, which is the cause of so many accidents to riders, can also have many causes. In the case of young horses. or those that have just come out of a stable, bucking can just be a sign of exuberance and enthusiasm. It usually stops after one or two hops. This also often occurs at the start of the first canter when out hacking, when riding across stubble fields or when in a larger group of horses. There is only one thing that helps – hold on tight, grab a piece of the mane, stick your knees into the knee rolls, go into a light seat and smile.

More often however bucking is a sign of pain. When bucking, a horse can loosen up its lumbar muscles that tense when the horse is in pain. If it can't relieve any unpleasant feeling after one or two bucks then it will at least get rid of the pesky burden on board.

Mental overload or a reluctance to work can be another cause of bucking and whether these causes lead to a horse bucking will depend on the horse's temperament and its level of suffering.

Bucking
I take it very seriously when my horses buck, which they do only very rarely, because my ponies have always expressed physical pain by bucking. Recently my cheeky pony, Lasse, who was always good to ride bareback, suddenly bucked when being mounted one day. The first time I thought the pony was just being cheeky and using it as a way to get out of work which he does often try to do. However after a careful examination by my chiropractor we determined that Lasset had kidney problems and bucking was how he could express his pain.

Especially amongst pony breeds there are those that have learnt – without any physical reasons whatsoever – to get rid of their riders very cleverly – either by bucking or coming to an abrupt halt.

The pony's eyes are calm, the ears are pricked and its nostrils show that it is being naughty rather than displaying fear.

When a horse, such as here, tries to evade the rider's aids by rearing then there are serious grounds for worry and the reasons should be investigated quickly and thoroughly.

Rearing

Rearing, which can after all look very impressive, is frequently a deliberately taught reaction when, on command of its rider, the horse goes up more or less vertically into the air. This is an exercise that is controlled and can be called up when the correct command is given. Once learned however, over-eager horses may use it as a creative distraction from something they may find harder to do or as displacement behaviour.

Many horses use rearing to avoid demands being made on them and it is also a sign of pain. They are however risking their own lives in doing so as uncontrolled, fearful or aggressive rearing can put them in danger of going over backwards and breaking their necks. It isn't for nothing that many trainers refuse to work with horses that have learnt to rear as a way of getting out of work. At the first signs of this occurring, such as lifting one or both front feet off the ground, it should be taken very seriously and the causes should be investigated.

The exception to this is blood stallions as they count rearing as part of their standard repertoire. Even here though you should be careful and ensure that you have some control.

Kicking

As a rider you will experience kicking usually when two horses meet or when they are going alongside each other. It gets especially dangerous when the animals are slightly offset to one another so that the rider's leg enters the target zone. This is why when riding in an arena with others, there should always be a horse's length between you and the rider in front. This is for safety rather than aesthetic reasons.

Horses indicate their aggression and intention to kick by laid-back ears and a look as if they are going to bite. If a rider doesn't do something at this stage then it's almost their own fault. The rider of the kicker must get their horse under control either by using their voice to get the horse's attention or by using other aids to get its attention back – either by leg yielding for a couple of steps, more contact or driving it forwards. With a horse that is showing clear signs of kicking or biting I think it is counterproductive to use a whip since the reaction is usually even more aggression from the horse.

Kicking can however also be a direct response to a rider's leg or to spurs that have been used too strongly. The horse may be indicating that it is experiencing pain when the rider's leg comes in contact with its totally cramped stomach muscles. More often however it is just a sign of resistance. Rather than passively avoiding the task by simply not reacting, the horse is meeting the problem with active resistance. Often kicking is a precursor to bucking and can be a warning of things to come.

This is a dangerous situation that is often underestimated. Both horses are threatening the other with clearly laid-back ears and teeth shown. An exchange of kicks is virtually guaranteed.

Tail-swishing

Alongside the ears and facial expression, the tail is one of the most used means for expressing pain or resistance. Tension in the back and loins is most clearly shown by a frantically waving tail. Tail-swishing belongs to very advanced movements, such as the piaffe, since it demands such a high inner degree of tension from the horse. If it turns into a propeller-like movement with the tail virtually going round and round then this is a sign of mental tension as well. Watch how often you see this in high level dressage. It has nothing at all to do with the suppleness and relaxedness that is supposed to be an essential element of dressage. In my opinion the riders should actually be disqualified rather than winning medals. Relaxedness and suppleness does after all come second to rhythm on the scale of training!

In the case of a horse that is working in a relaxed and supple way the tail should swing in time to the movement. It is always a sign of a loose, swinging back and a mentally relaxed horse.

For vets and osteopaths, when the tail is held crookedly this is a sign that the horse's skeleton may be crooked or its muscles may not be evenly developed. Many animals will carry the tail clearly to the left or right – even without the rider doing anything. If this is the case you should clarify whether there is a problem or whether the horse has just been born that way.

Tense steps and a propeller tail – the entire horse is a picture of tension. This is not a picture of harmony and suppleness, and yet the horse was placed...

The same pace but a totally different picture. Here we have a relaxed, swinging tail, a calm expression and a horse that is striding out in front and through its back.

Head-tossing

Head-tossing can indicate many problems. Head-tossing is an expression of unwillingness or reluctance even between herd members and the same applies to a horse doing this when being ridden. It will also do this when it doesn't want to do a particular movement or is feeling overtaxed.

More often tossing the head is a sign of physical pain, for example when the rider is too strong in the hand or when they apply the aids too strongly and cause pain. There are riders who have even broken a horse's jaw... Sometimes though an unsteady or insecure hand can cause a horse to toss its head. When a young horse is looking for a contact to better establish its balance and only finds a loose or floppy rein it may start to toss its head. The inexperienced rider thinks that it is pulling the reins and so lets go even more. A quiet and steady contact though would solve the problem. This is why I would always suggest that an inexperienced horse belongs in an experienced rider's hands!

Pain during tooth growth or when there are teeth or jaw problems is also often the cause of head-tossing when a horse is being ridden, just as unsuitable or painful bits are. The width of the jaw and the thickness of its tongue will vary from horse to horse. You need therefore to check carefully whether new bits really do fit, rather than just using them because they are fashionable. It is best to ask your vet to check for any problems.

Head-tossing can also come from a tense back or neck or from spinal problems since everything is connected. My experience has shown that head-tossing or worse is usually preceded by feeling some sort of stiffness on one side when riding.

Natural crookedness

Every horse will prefer to go on one rein more than the other. This is exactly the same as our right- or left-handedness. Once it was thought that this came from the position in the mother's womb but today it is more put down to the preference of position in which a foal grazes, when it puts one leg in front and the other back – it is usually always the same one that is put forwards. Sometimes though we ride this one-sidedness into our horses since we ourselves tend to be either very right- or left-handed and we carry over our own crookedness to our horses by continuously giving them the aids unevenly.

In summer many owners find that their horses toss their heads even more due to a hypersensitivity to insects or a kind of allergic reaction that is sometimes called head shaking. A further cause of this can also be a hypersensitivity to sunlight experienced in the nasal passage and nostrils. Nose nets are now available that you can attach to the bridle and these often help to solve part or all of the problem. Regardless of whether it is the flies or the sun – for sensitive animals like these it is a good idea to always ride them in a fly mask that absorbs ultraviolet and so create a better working environment for both horse and rider.

This horse's head has been pulled onto its chest with its mouth shut tight. It has no chance to relieve the pressure on its tongue and jaw. Its face is tense and the eye resigned. It is trying to relieve its plight by tossing and nodding its head.

The horse's mouth

If all horses could move their mouths as they wanted a shocking number would go through life as riding horses with their mouths wide open. It is only the noseband in its many permutations that prevents this by closing it tight. Due to the sometimes painful effect of the bit the horse will bite its tongue or try to stick it out. Some horses have their tongues squeezed so much that they turn blue – how are you supposed to achieve suppleness when a horse is faced with this?

It shocks me again and again how so many riders tighten up their horse's noseband as much as they can without thinking about it – sometimes with the even greater pressure which you get from a crank noseband. If a horse has to have its mouth pulled shut surely it is time to ask yourself why? Is the hand too hard, the bit unsuitable or too strong? Is the movement too difficult? Are the other aids not clear enough which mean that the hand has to do more? Your horse's mouth will tell you all of this – if it is given a chance.

There is a reason for the saying, "Always ride your horse from back to front". The leg and seat aids should always come first before the hand. The horse's head shouldn't be pulled onto its chest as is seen all too often. Instead a horse should engage its hind legs and work over its back. When the rider's hand then offers a steady and safe contact the horse will come onto it and by taking more weight onto its quarters it will flex through the poll, come onto the bit and be in the rider's hands.

It isn't always the rider's hand or a tightly fastened noseband that causes a horse to be unsettled in its mouth. Many thoroughbred horses compensate for their inner tension through an extremely mobile mouth. They tend to chew a lot and produce a lot of foam around the mouth, sometimes even grinding or snapping their teeth as a further sign of stress. It might not always be negative stress, but can also be a sign of over-eagerness. You can tell the difference by the expression in the eyes and the movement of the tail.

A tense upper lip is also a sign of tension or exertion. A sensitive rider can feel a tense mouth through their hands since tense muscles in the head have an effect on the poll which will make any dialogue with your horse stiffer and more tense.

Lack of space: The horse's mouth is tied shut with two nosebands with the combination bit pulled as far as it goes. But it is the eye that really shows the pain.

This is what the relaxed mouth of a happy horse looks like. There is nothing restricting. The foam indicates a good level of movement in the mouth.

Noises –
teeth grinding, groaning and sheath noises

Some horses really do grind their teeth when being ridden – with or without a bit in the mouth. Getting them to let go and relax though is something quite different. Often the grinding of teeth has become a pattern of behaviour that the horse does automatically because it has become so firmly established. If you change the work it can take some time until the grinding or the snapping of teeth, which is when horses almost seem to chatter with their teeth, stops as they have to first get used to the new and more beneficial way of working.

Many horses grunt or groan from exertion – physical and mental. It may be that the rider is simply too heavy for the horse or that the horse just has problems with its body in a particular movement. Either it isn't supple enough for the movement or it really is just finding it hard work. In addition groaning can of course also be an indication of real pain.

By their very nature only geldings and stallions can make sheath noises and they are usually a sign of stress and tension since they usually only occur when the animal has tense or cramped stomach muscles. How much they are also a sign of pain has not been sufficiently researched.

> **Blowing out through the nose**
> We should always remember that horses – just like us – regulate their tension through their breathing. Tense horses hold their breath which results in the stomach muscles being tensed. If the tension is relieved then they will breathe out and snort gently. This is why, when warming your horse up, you should pay attention to whether, as it becomes increasingly supple, it releases its breath and blows out with a gentle and prolonged snorting noise, and praise it when it does. It is a sign that it is starting to relax and trust you.

Finding the right support

I could of course go on to deal with every imaginable situation that occurs with horses and detail their emotional significance and how it relates to communication – but this really isn't necessary. At the end of the day the same sort of patterns of behaviour happen over and over again. You just have to be prepared to take the time to learn to notice and interpret them and when handling or involved with horses always to concentrate on keeping an eye on the overall situation. If you already have communication problems with your horse then you should seek help – even if it costs a bit of money. Choose a trainer though who specifically offers in-hand work and doesn't just use hard methods. A glance through the trainer's yard, a look in his or her horses' eyes and the mood that prevails will often tell you more than a thousand promises.

When dealing with horses you have to be consistent and be comfortable about being assertive. Horses aren't cuddly toys and they aren't always harmless. I have had to use physical strength with some horses to make them pay attention and take me seriously and it's been enough to make a layman flinch. It is all about reacting appropriately. It is pointless to be intentionally aggressive towards an insecure or frightened horse when only calmness and building trust will work. In the case of a cheeky horse though I don't give it too long to respond and instead I have to be faster to put pressure on and demand immediate obedience. To be able to distinguish what is needed requires experience and ability.

Look around at other disciplines in case you can find real horse people there too who have their horses' trust. You can recognise a good horseman from the way his horses are – they become well-behaved apparently by themselves and do what is asked of them without effort. Everything looks easy. The horse likes being with him and seeks out his presence. Watch very carefully how such people work with their horses and open your heart – it is much wiser than you think …

It isn't just the technical expertise that makes a trainer good but rather their ability to establish a good personal relationship with you.

Acknowledgements

I would like to give a big thank you to all the trainers who work with their hearts and offer their expertise to make those of us who are thirsty for knowledge more knowledgeable about the nature of horses. And those too who go to the effort of writing about their knowledge and/or stand out in the wind and cold to teach us. To list them all would become a who's who of the training world and I have never been one for boasting, even during my time as a journalist.

I would however like to mention two names since they haven't merely helped me put this book together but have always been there for me and my horses with their enormous expertise. One is Gunnar Örn Isleifsson, a fantastic horseman – a trainer and equine dentist. The other is my riding instructor, Regina Johannsen, who is always telling me to use my senses more and observe carefully when working with my horses.

And of course I need to thank my ponies who give me new insights into their world on a daily basis and show so much patience towards me and my pupils and help them on their way to becoming understanding horsemen and women. You are the best! Thank you to my Andalusian, Valeroso; Arab cross, Laurin; the Fjord ponies, Mali, Eric, Hanne and Sunny; the Koniks, Baschka and Grazina; Lewitzer-cross, Tulkas; Haflinger-cross, Hansl; "dwarf" Andalusian, Pretty and her daughter Pearl; the Shetland ponies, Rocky, Stöpsel, Lasse, Jasper, Brownie, Maja, Toni, Fiete, Laika, Picasso, Jimmy and Moses (photos can be seen on www.ponyschule. info) – and all of the horses on which I have been privileged to learn to ride and that have had to suffer my incompetence and quest for knowledge.

Thanks too to Christiane Slawik, without whose wonderful photos this book would not have been possible. During the hectic final phase of putting this book together she was travelling around the world on the hunt for new photos. She too would like to thank all of the horses who have opened their souls to her.

125

Appendix

Bibliography

Wendt, Marlitt:
Trust Instead of Dominance – Working towards
a new form of ethical horsemanship:
Cadmos Publishing 2011

Wendt, Marlitt:
How Horses Feel and Think – Understanding
behavior, emotions and intelligence:
Cadmos Publishing 2011

Weritz, Linda
Horse Sense and Horsemanship
Ranking, Partnership, Energy transfer
Cadmos Publishing 2008

Index

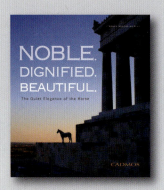

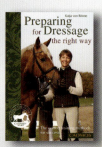